WITHDRAWN

STONEWALL JACKSON

STONEWALL JACKSON

A Biography

Ethan S. Rafuse

GREENWOOD BIOGRAPHIES

GREENWOOD

AN IMPRINT OF ABC-CLIO, LLC
Santa Barbara, California • Denver, Colorado • Oxford, England

Library of Congress Cataloging-in-Publication Data

Rafuse, Ethan Sepp, 1968–
  Stonewall Jackson : a biography / Ethan S. Rafuse.
      p. cm. — (Greenwood biographies)
  Includes bibliographical references and index.
  ISBN 978-0-313-38583-4 (hardcopy : alk. paper) — ISBN 978-0-313-38584-1 (ebook)   1. Jackson, Stonewall, 1824–1863.   2. Generals—United States—Biography.   3. Confederate States of America. Army—Officers—Biography. 4. Shenandoah Valley Campaign, 1861.   5. Shenandoah Valley Campaign, 1862.   6. United States—History—Civil War, 1861–1865—Campaigns.   I. Title.
  E467.1.J15R19   2011
  973.7'3092—dc22
  [B]   2011010012

ISBN: 978-0-313-38583-4
EISBN: 978-0-313-38584-1

15 14 13 12 11   1 2 3 4 5

This book is also available on the World Wide Web as an eBook.
Visit www.abc-clio.com for details.

ABC-CLIO, LLC
130 Cremona Drive, P.O. Box 1911
Santa Barbara, California 93116-1911

This book is printed on acid-free paper ∞

Manufactured in the United States of America

To Rachel and Corinne

CONTENTS

CONTENTS

SERIES FOREWORD

In response to high school and public library needs, Greenwood developed this distinguished series of full-length biographies specifically for student use. Prepared by field experts and professionals, these engaging biographies are tailored for high school students who need challenging yet accessible biographies. Ideal for secondary school assignments, the length, format and subject areas are designed to meet educators' requirements and students' interests.

Greenwood offers an extensive selection of biographies spanning all curriculum related subject areas including social studies, the sciences, literature and the arts, history and politics, as well as popular culture, covering public figures and famous personalities from all time periods and backgrounds, both historic and contemporary, who have made an impact on American and/or world culture. Greenwood biographies were chosen based on comprehensive feedback from librarians and educators. Consideration was given to both curriculum relevance and inherent interest. The result is an intriguing mix of the well known and the unexpected, the saints and sinners from long-ago history and contemporary pop culture. Readers will find a wide array of subject choices from fascinating crime figures like Al Capone to inspiring pioneers like Margaret Mead, from the greatest minds of our time like Stephen Hawking to the most amazing success stories of our day like J.K. Rowling.

While the emphasis is on fact, not glorification, the books are meant to be fun to read. Each volume provides in-depth information about the subject's life from birth through childhood, the teen years, and adulthood. A thorough account relates family background and education, traces personal and professional influences, and explores struggles, accomplishments, and contributions. A timeline highlights the most significant life events against a historical perspective. Bibliographies supplement the reference value of each volume.

PREFACE

At the time of his death in May 1863, perhaps no military man stood higher in the estimation of the American public—in both the North and South—than Thomas Jonathan "Stonewall" Jackson. His performances in 1861 and 1862 at such battles as First Manassas, Fredericksburg, and Chancellorsville were critical to the ability of outnumbered Confederate armies to achieve victories and brought him worldwide fame. The brilliant campaign he conducted in the Shenandoah Valley in the spring of 1862 was critical to the survival of the Confederate cause in Virginia in 1862 and remains a source of valuable lessons and inspiration to students of military history. Later that same year, he commanded an operation at Harpers Ferry that ended with the surrender of nearly 12,000 U.S. soldiers—an accomplishment that would not be matched for 80 years.

Indeed, Jackson's death is often seen as the point when the winds of fortune turned against the South in its bid for independence. Prior to that event, the Confederate war effort in the East (it was a quite different story west of the Appalachian Mountains) achieved a truly impressive series of battlefield victories against what seemed on paper to be overwhelming odds. These victories were to a large extent a product of Jackson's ruthlessly aggressive approach to war, an approach characterized by fast marching, bold risk taking, skillfully conceived maneuvers, and resolutely delivered attacks. Indeed, "Stonewall," the nickname attached to Jackson, while appropriate given the situation on the battlefield when it was bestowed, may well have been the most ironic in all of American military history.

Even had the Civil War never occurred, Jackson's story would still be one worthy of retelling, for it is in many ways a classic American "rags to riches" tale. Born into obscurity in the rugged mountains of western Virginia, the sort of opportunities enjoyed by many Americans of his age—not the least those who would become his classmates at the U.S. Military Academy at West Point, peers in the U.S. Army and at the Virginia Military Institute, and colleagues and enemies in the Civil War—were largely absent from Jackson's early life. Nonetheless, seizing on a remarkable stroke of good fortune, Jackson secured a much-coveted appointment to West Point. There Jackson overcame what he lacked in preparatory schooling through self-discipline, grit, and determination to complete the rigorous program of studies at the military academy. He then served with distinction as a junior officer in the Mexican War, impressing his peers and superiors with the ability and courage with which he executed his duties under fire. Unable to find satisfaction in peacetime army duties, a few years later he accepted a teaching position at the Virginia Military Institute, where he taught many of the young men he would lead to victory in battle during the first two years of the Civil War.

As if Jackson's remarkable military career were not enough to ensure that his story would attract attention from posterity, there also is the fact that Jackson was a truly fascinating individual from a personal standpoint. Indeed, Jackson's prominent place in the hearts and minds of Americans, especially in the South, is also attributable to his personal character, which was distinguished by iron self-discipline, a quirky inclination toward what some may have seen as hypochondria, toughness of mind, and, above all, a powerful commitment to his Christian faith. Although it did not keep him from regularly sleeping in church, Jackson's faith was at the core of his character, something he pursued rigorously and that guided his life. This aspect of Jackson's character especially resonated with the people of the Confederate South, who saw in his story and character their own dedication to faith and family, commitment to the cause of victory, and ability to persevere against long odds—as well as their destiny to fall short in their bid for final victory.

For these reasons, in the 150 years since his death, Jackson's legend has not diminished. Of all the men who commanded Confederate troops, only Robert E. Lee enjoys a higher degree of enduring fame and respect from students of military history and the general public. Jackson's place in the southern mind is reflected in the many sites in Maryland, West Virginia, and Virginia that are dedicated to honoring and preserving the memory of the man and his accomplishments as a soldier. It is evident in his inclusion, along with Lee and Confederate president Jefferson Davis, in the largest bas relief sculpture in the world, the Confederate Memorial Carving on Stone Mountain in Georgia. It is reflected in the innumerable authors and artists who have found Jackson an irresistibly compelling subject, and the large audience their works have attracted. Not least, it was evident in the 2003 motion picture *Gods and Generals*, which recreates (with some artistic license) the experiences of a number of prominent commanders during the first two years of war, but in which it is Jackson's story that receives the most attention.

This effort to tell Jackson's story benefited immeasurably from the support and encouragement I received from numerous people, and it is my great pleasure to express my appreciation here. As always, first among these are my wife Rachel and daughter Corinne, whose love and encouragement were critical in so many ways to completion of this project. So too was the relocation of members of the Rafuse tribe to Rawley Springs a few years ago, which did much to diminish the logistical challenge studying the battlefields of the Shenandoah Valley can present. I am also appreciative for the support I have received from members of one of the finest communities of scholars and teachers of military history in the world at the U.S. Army Command and General Staff College, above all department chair James H. Willbanks. Three of this generation's truly outstanding scholars of the Civil War, Gary Ecelbarger, Frank O'Reilly, and Brooks Simpson, read earlier drafts of the manuscript and provided many invaluable (and much appreciated) suggestions for its improvement. I am also thankful for the many friends and colleagues, such as Ed Bearss, Terry Beckenbaugh, Charles Bowery, Tom Clemens, Christian Keller, Curt King, Dana Mangham, Michael Miller, Randy Mullis, Carol Reardon, Christopher Stowe, Samuel Watson, Jeff Wert, and Brad Wineman, who over the years have collaborated with me on tours and staff rides of the battlefields where Stonewall Jackson won fame during the Civil War.

TIMELINE: EVENTS IN THE LIFE OF STONEWALL JACKSON

1824, January 21	Born in Clarksburg, Virginia.
1842, June	Enters U.S. Military Academy at West Point, New York.
1846, June	Graduates from U.S. Military Academy and receives commission as brevet second lieutenant of artillery.
1847, March	Sees first combat action at Vera Cruz, Mexico.
1847, August 19	Distinguishes himself at the Battle of Contreras.
1847, September 12	Performs with distinction during U.S. assault on Chapultepec.
1849, April 29	Baptized at St. John's Episcopal Church in New York City.
1851, August 13	Reports for duty at Virginia Military Institute in Lexington, Virginia.
1852, February 20	Resigns commission in U.S. Army.
1853, August 4	Marries Elinor "Ellie" Junkin in Lexington, Virginia.

1854, October 22	Son is delivered stillborn; Ellie dies from related complications.
1857, July 16	Marries Mary Anna Morrison.
1859, December 2	Witnesses execution of abolitionist John Brown.
1861, April 17	Virginia convention votes to secede from the Union.
1861, April 26	Appointed colonel in Virginia armed forces.
1861, April 29	Assumes command at Harpers Ferry.
1861, May 23	Superseded by Joseph Johnston in command at Harpers Ferry.
1861, July 2	Engagement at Falling Waters.
1861, July 3	Learns of promotion to brigadier general in the Confederate Army.
1861, July 21	First Battle of Manassas (Bull Run), performance inspires nickname of "Stonewall."
1861, October 7	Promotion to major general.
1861, November 5	Assumes command of Valley District.
1862, January 1–14	Romney Campaign.
1862, March 23	First Battle of Kernstown.
1862, May 8	Battle of McDowell.
1862, May 23	Battle of Front Royal.
1862, May 25	First Battle of Winchester.
1862, June 8	Battle of Cross Keys.
1862, June 9	Battle of Port Republic.
1862, June 17–18	Leaves Shenandoah Valley to participate in defense of Richmond.
1862, June 26	Battle of Mechanicsville (Beaver Dam Creek).
1862, June 27	Battle of Gaines' Mill.
1862, June 30	Battle of White Oak Swamp (Glendale).
1862, July 1	Battle of Malvern Hill.
1862, August 9	Battle of Cedar Mountain.
1862, August 28–30	Second Battle of Manassas (Bull Run).
1862, September 1	Battle of Ox Hill (Chantilly).
1862, September 15	Captures Harpers Ferry.
1862, September 17	Battle of Antietam (Sharpsburg).
1862, September 19	Battle of Shepherdstown.

1862, October 10	Promotion to lieutenant general.
1862, November	Jackson's command is organized into the Second Corps, Army of Northern Virginia.
1862, November 28	Learns of birth of daughter Julia in Charlotte, North Carolina.
1862, December 13	Battle of Fredericksburg.
1862, December–March 1863	Makes winter headquarters at Moss Neck Plantation.
1863, April 20–29	Anna and Julia visit headquarters near Fredericksburg, Virginia.
1863, April–May 5	Chancellorsville Campaign.
1863, May 2	Suffers wounds while conducting a nighttime reconnaissance west of Chancellorsville.
1863, May 3	Left arm amputated at Second Corps field hospital near Wilderness Tavern.
1863, May 4	Relocation from Wilderness Tavern to Chandler Plantation near Guinea Station.
1863, May 10	Dies of pneumonia at Chandler Plantation.
1863, May 15	Burial in family plot in Lexington, Virginia.

Chapter 1

MAKING OF A SOLDIER

COMING OF AGE IN WESTERN VIRGINIA

Few episodes in American history have been so rich in ironies and curiosities as the Civil War. Thus, it is perhaps not so curious that the remarkable man who was one of the most feared Confederate commanders hailed from a section of Virginia that so objected to the cause of Confederate independence that it seceded from Virginia in 1863 and created the new state of West Virginia. But this indeed was the case.

Nestled in the rugged mountains of western Virginia, Clarksburg was still a fairly new and rough little hamlet when, shortly after marrying Julia Beckwith Neale on September 28, 1817, Jonathan Jackson decided to stake his future on the place. Like so many others of sturdy Scots-Irish descent, the Jackson family had first set down roots in western Virginia in the 1750s. It was 1755 when John and Elizabeth Cummins Jackson married after completing the period of indenture a pair of London courts determined would be their punishment for larceny. The two had met on the prison ship that carried them to the New World, fell in love, and, after earning their freedom, made their way west over the Blue Ridge and Shenandoah Valley to settle in Moorefield, Virginia. By the 1770s, they had resettled to the Tygart River valley and began acquiring land. During the American War for Independence, John further enhanced his stature in the community by serving the patriot cause as a captain. After completing his military service, he continued to energetically pursue his own economic interest, acquiring vast tracts of land and slaves, while also serving his local community in a number of public offices.

John's second son Edward, born in 1759, also found prosperity as a surveyor and engineer, aided by a strategic marriage to Mary Hadden, the offspring of a prominent Randolph County family. After Mary's death in 1796, Edward relocated to the young town of Clarksburg, remarried, and followed his father's lead in acquiring substantial land holdings. The most significant of these developed into the town of Weston, which Jackson would serve as a justice of the peace and in a number of other significant public offices.

In 1810 Edward Jackson's 20-year-old third son, Jonathan, was admitted to the bar in Clarksburg. Jonathan followed his grandfather's path when war with Britain came again in 1812, earning a commission as a lieutenant in a cavalry company he helped recruit. His subsequent career as a lawyer and in business would not be marked, though, with the kind of success that his father and grandfather had enjoyed. He quickly fell deeply in debt, due in part to his fondness for poker and alcohol. Despite marriage in 1817 to Julia Beckwith Neale, the daughter of a prosperous Parkersburg merchant, and the prominence the family enjoyed in Clarksburg society, Jonathan Jackson's defects of character were such that he never stopped struggling professionally and financially. In 1819, their first child, a daughter, was born, followed two years later by a son. During the night of January 20–21, 1824, their third child was born, a son, whom they named Thomas Jonathan Jackson.

Two years later, tragedy struck. In 1826, Jonathan's and Julia's eldest child was stricken with typhoid fever and died. Shortly thereafter, on March 26, Jonathan succumbed to typhoid. His and Julia's fourth child was born the following day, leaving Jonathan's widow Julia with three young children to raise. As if this were not enough to ensure a hard road lay ahead, Julia was forced to sell the house to cover the debts

Jonathan had accumulated. She then moved the family into a one-room house and took up sewing and teaching to support the family, battling poverty while suffering through what would be a persistent and ultimately fatal bout with tuberculosis.

Remarriage to Blake B. Woodson in November 1830 did little to improve the situation. Woodson, like Jonathan, was the product of a prominent family whose record of accomplishment he fell far short of sustaining. Even an appointment to be clerk of the court for newly organized Fayette County proved insufficient to reverse the decline in Woodson's fortunes, and his already powerful sense of bitterness and self-loathing, which he took out on his and Julia's children, only increased. By the time Thomas was seven, the family's financial situation was so dire, and his mother's health had declined to such a point, that it was decided to send him and his sister Laura to Jackson's Mill, a 1,500-acre tract of land north of Weston where they could be taken care of by other members of the extended Jackson family.

After a heart-rending parting with his mother, a week-long trek through the western Virginia wilderness brought Thomas and his sister to Jackson's Mill. They were quickly welcomed into a large band of Jackson relatives, but before they had completely settled in, they had to make a return trek to Fayette County to see their mother, who had just given birth to a son, an ordeal that left the physically frail woman at death's door. Jackson arrived in time to see his mother and receive one last blessing from her before she died on December 4, 1831, leaving him and his siblings orphans.

After the question of the fate of Julia's children was settled by placing them under the care of the family at Jackson's Mill, Thomas spent four years contributing to the family enterprise there, over which his uncle Cummins Jackson presided. He learned the skills associated with life on a farm under the supervision of his extended family, developing a love of farming and demonstrating such natural skill with the horses his uncle bred and raised for the racetrack that he eventually became his uncle's lead jockey. Then, in August 1835, the matriarch of Jackson's Mill died. With no female figure there to raise the children, it was decided to send Laura and Thomas elsewhere. Laura would go to Parkersburg to live with the Neale family, while 12-year-old Thomas would be taken in by an aunt and uncle who lived near Clarksburg.

This arrangement did not last long. Thomas's uncle was a rough, hard-driving man, who both verbally and physically abused his nephew. Unable to endure the situation, Thomas ran away and informed family members in Clarksburg there was no way he would return to his uncle and aunt. He then made his way back to Jackson's Mill, where he was welcomed back by his bachelor uncles and returned to work there.

The grandest adventure of Jackson's early life, though, began in 1836 when his older brother, Warren, who was working as a schoolteacher in Upshur County, invited him to come along on a trip to Parkersburg. Excited at the prospect of seeing his sister again, Thomas eagerly accepted and was easily persuaded after reaching Parkersburg to participate in a scheme Warren had hatched to travel down the Ohio River and make money selling firewood to steamboats. Thus, during the spring of 1836, 15-year-old Warren and 12-year-old Thomas departed Parkersburg and made their way down the Ohio until they reached the Mississippi River, where they set up operations on a small island near the shore of Kentucky. Their enterprise floundered, however, when both boys fell ill with malaria and decided to return to Virginia. Thanks in part to the generosity of a steamboat captain, Warren and Thomas were able to return to Virginia in early 1837. Warren, though, would never fully recover physically from the ordeal, and lingering effects of the malaria would contribute to his death less than five years later.

Even before his trip down the Ohio, Thomas had developed a powerful desire to pursue an education. Uncle Cummins, although initially skeptical regarding his nephew's prospects outside the racetrack, nonetheless managed to get a small school established at Jackson's Mill. Thomas began his studies with enthusiasm, and it was soon clear that learning was something he greatly enjoyed and valued. By the end of 1837, he was regularly attending classes taught for free in Weston. Jackson then continued his studies under local scholar Alexander Scott Withers and lawyer Matthew Edmiston and quickly became close to both men. Jackson's prospects further brightened when his uncle secured him a temporary position as an engineering assistant on a project to build a turnpike connecting Parkersburg and Staunton, Virginia, in which his already evident interest and natural talent for mathematics was further developed. Jackson also took advantage of an offer from the family of his friend Joseph Lightburn that he could borrow books from their library. He and Joseph subsequently developed a particular interest in a book on Francis Marion, whose exploits as a leader of irregular forces in the Carolinas during the Revolution won him the nickname the "Swamp Fox."

Jackson also came into contact during this time with the Bible and began to develop a strong interest in religion. This was something that had not been a major factor in the lives of some members of his family, but increasingly it would be for Jackson in the following years. By 1841, he was praying nightly, taking advantage of the Lightburns' invitation to attend the Broad Run Baptist Church near their farm, and also attending services at a Methodist Church in Weston.

These experiences led Jackson to give considerable thought to becoming a minister during his teenage years. However, in 1840 his scholastic efforts had led to an invitation to teach school near Jackson's Mill. Jackson accepted and proceeded to spend three months working with a small class of three girls and two boys. That same year Jackson also began to experience periodic bouts of severe abdominal pain, the most persistent of the many physical problems he would battle throughout his adult life.

Shortly thereafter, in June 1841, the 17-year-old Jackson received an appointment as constable for a large section of Lewis County, a position he would hold for 10 months. When this job was over, the question of what Jackson would do with his future was a decidedly open one. Fortuitously, in 1840, a member of his extended family named Samuel L. Hays had been elected to the U.S. Congress. Shortly after entering office, Hays announced that he was looking for candidates for an appointment to the U.S. Military Academy at West Point, New York. Almost immediately, both Jackson and his friend Joseph Lightburn expressed interest. Soon, though, Lightburn dropped out, leaving Jackson's only significant competition Gibson J. Butcher, a resident of Weston with whom he was already well-acquainted. Jackson did all he could to advance his prospects for receiving the appointment, but in April 1842, it was announced that it would go to Butcher.

Jackson was understandably devastated and was left to ponder what must have seemed at the time to be a rather bleak menu of future prospects. Then, a few short months later, events took a sudden and welcome turn. Less than 48 hours after arriving at West Point in

June 1842 and receiving his first taste of the rigorous discipline that characterized life at the military academy, Butcher decided he had made a serious mistake in accepting the appointment and was on his way back to Weston. When Butcher reached Weston, an immediate effort was organized to petition Hays to give the just-opened slot at the academy to Jackson.

A flurry of activity followed, involving a delighted Jackson and numerous residents of Weston negotiating the various hoops that stood between him and West Point. There was an interview with prominent local attorney Jonathan Bennett to persuade him to write a letter of recommendation to Hays on Jackson's behalf. Bennett bluntly asked whether Jackson "did not fear that his education was not sufficient to enable him to enter and sustain himself at West Point." "I know," Jackson replied, "I shall have the application necessary to succeed; I hope that I have the capacity; at least, I am determined to try, and I want you to help me." Impressed with Jackson's determination, Bennett agreed to support his efforts. As Bennett did what he could to help his candidacy, Jackson also received a brief, albeit rigorous tutoring in spelling and grammar from his former instructors Edmiston and Withers to prepare himself for the entrance examinations that awaited him at the academy.

Jackson then traveled by horse, stagecoach, and locomotive to Washington for what would be another whirlwind of activity. Upon arriving in the capital on June 17, Jackson made his way to the office of Congressman Hays. There he became the first person to inform the congressman of what had become of the young man he had appointed to West Point a few months back, when he handed him Butcher's letter of resignation. Jackson also showed Hays the many petitions from home urging that he be given Butcher's place. Hays then took up his pen to write to the secretary of war informing him of what had transpired. He apologized for what had happened with Butcher and requested that Jackson be authorized to take his place at the academy. On June 18, the secretary of war officially granted conditional appointment to the U.S. Military Academy to Thomas J. Jackson.

Declining an invitation from Hays to spend a few days in Washington, Jackson immediately secured transportation for the trip to West Point. On June 19, Jackson stepped off the Hudson River ferryboat that had taken him from New York City to West Point. He then made his way up the bluff to the famous plain overlooking the river on which the academy was situated and caught his first glimpse of the place he hoped would be his home for the next four years.

WEST POINT

Whether this hope would be realized was an open question, though. First, Jackson had to make it through a series of physical and academic examinations so the academy could determine whether it should even bother letting him begin the program. That Thomas Jackson was a decidedly determined young man was made evident to at least one of his fellow cadets on the very first day he was at West Point. When Jackson first approached the barracks to which he had been assigned that day, he immediately attracted the attention of three new cadets from Virginia, Dabney Maury, Birkett Fry, and Ambrose Powell Hill. All three would become generals in the Confederate army, but in 1842 they were complete strangers to Jackson. All of them also had received far better educations and introductions to the social graces that defined proper society than Jackson. They could hardly have been more different in this regard from the rough-hewn, shabbily dressed, and unsociable fellow from western Virginia approaching them. Nonetheless, Maury perceived there was something more in Jackson than a mere hick from the mountains. "That fellow," he remarked to his associates, "looks as if he has come to stay."

Maury also decided that this new fellow could use a friend to help him adjust to his new situation. Finding himself and Jackson assigned the task of policing the barracks, Maury tried to strike up a lighthearted conversation. Jackson, whose natural reticence was no doubt exacerbated by an acute sensitivity to the contrast between himself and his new associates—not to mention a degree of exhaustion from all he had gone through the past few weeks just to get to West Point, would have none of it. He received Maury's efforts with a cold stare. Thinking that perhaps he had been too forward and presuming in his initial approach, Maury later went up to Jackson and apologized if the "playful" tone with which he had earlier spoke had been out of line and "not justified by our slight acquaintance." Once again, Jackson curtly rebuffed

Maury. Furious, Maury shortly thereafter advised some of their fellow cadets that there was no point in making any effort to be social with such a "jackass" as "Cadet Jackson, from Virginia."

Undoubtedly weighing much more heavily on Jackson's mind than the good opinion of Maury and the rest of the corps of cadets at that point were the entrance examinations that came three days after he arrived at West Point. Jackson's nervousness was evident to one cadet who witnessed his effort to solve a mathematics problem. "When he went to the blackboard the perspiration was streaming from his face," he later remembered, "and during the whole examination his anxiety was painful to witness. While trying to work his example in fractions, the cuffs of his coat, first the right and then the left, were brought in to requisition to wipe off the perspiration." Jackson, though, not only managed to answer the problem correctly, but also demonstrated in the course of his examinations that his reading and writing ability were sufficient to enable him to continue the program.

Still, this accomplishment hardly ensured Jackson a bright future at West Point. He had certainly done better than the 30 of his would-be fellow cadets who failed to pass the examinations. Nonetheless, when the list of 133 qualified cadets was officially posted on June 24, 1842, Jackson's name appeared dead last. Given that the classes tended to shed at least a third of their members over the course of the four-year program—and sometimes far more than that—it was clear that there was much cause for concern.

Of course, academics were but one aspect of the program at West Point. In July, Jackson and his fellow cadets moved out of their barracks and into summer encampment, where they began receiving instruction in military subjects. For weeks, they were subjected to a rigorous and uncomfortable experience dominated by drill, marching, and instruction in the manual of arms, all of which were designed to introduce them to the hard life of the 19th-century soldier. Whether Jackson and his classmates possessed the self-discipline to keep their uniforms and equipment in top condition was constantly checked, and as they struggled with the multitude of tasks associated with life in the field they were subjected to constant verbal abuse from the older cadets who ran the camps. There is no evidence that Jackson found the challenges of summer encampment in any way insurmountable, although he did pick up six demerits in its course for relatively minor infractions.

Still, his prospects for survival (much less success) at West Point did not appear so bright when the academic program began in September. Fortunately, Jackson seems to have had a natural facility at mathematics, the subject that dominated the curriculum at the military academy. Nonetheless, the deficiencies of his schooling prior to West Point relative to what most of the other cadets had experienced were evident. He found the program extremely difficult and by the end of the first month was already in serious trouble academically.

While he had training in basic arithmetic, Jackson had never before been exposed to such advanced subjects in mathematics as algebra and geometry. Nor had he had much experience with the French language, which, due to the high status of the French military in the minds of West Point's authorities, was a major part of the first year's curriculum. By the end of the first semester, with examinations looming in January, Jackson was already thinking about what he was going to say to his community when he became the second son West Point had sent home to western Virginia that year in failure.

What he might have lacked in preparation and natural genius, though, Jackson more than made up for in determination. While never popular personally, Jackson's conscientiousness and willingness to devote long hours to his studies quickly impressed his fellow cadets. These qualities enabled him to survive the January 1843 examinations, but in what would hardly be considered spectacular fashion. Of the members of his class still in the program (it had already shed another 32 members) Jackson ranked 71st—his standing boosted considerably by his lack of demerits for conduct. Nonetheless, this brought his probationary period at the academy to an end, and on February 20, 1843, he signed an oath of allegiance making him an official cadet at the U.S. Military Academy.

The second half of the 1842–43 academic year at West Point saw Jackson's persistence pay off, as he began steadily improving his academic performance and overall standing at the academy. As a result of the June 1843 examinations, he advanced 17 places in class rank in mathematics and 18 in French, while his conduct and military bearing remained exemplary. Still, Jackson saw no grounds for complacency. Unlike many of his classmates, who during their second year at the academy began engaging in the social and recreational activities available, Jackson eschewed them to focus on his studies. Nonetheless, he began developing friendships, was clearly respected by his fellow cadets, and became much warmer with them than his introduction to Maury had led them to expect. Still, he never became a particularly popular figure at the academy.

When he had free time, Jackson preferred to spend it walking around the post, taking in the spectacular scenery around West Point, which undoubtedly brought to his mind memories of his home in the mountains of western Virginia. One of his favorite spots was the ruins of Fort Putnam, which had been built during the American Revolution on a piece of high ground overlooking the plain. There he enjoyed both solitude and a spectacular view of the plain, the Hudson River, and the surrounding area. Privately, he began compiling in a notebook a list of rules and maxims to guide his conduct. "Perhaps the most characteristic of these," his wife later declared, "was '*You may be whatever you resolve to be.*'"

Nonetheless, he still found the academic program a considerable challenge. His performance in the January 1844 examinations once again led to a rise in his standing in mathematics—he now stood in the top third of the class—and in French. Yet Jackson now found himself near the bottom of the class in drawing. Moreover, he confessed in a letter to his sister Laura that month, "I am also homesick, and expect to continue so until I can have a view of my native mountains." Still, he was generally positive about his situation and justifiably proud of what he had achieved so far, adding, "My health is far better than it was when I parted with you, and indeed more flattering than it has been for the last two years. . . . I feel very confident that unless fortune frowns on me more than it has yet, I shall graduate in the upper half of my class."

In June 1844, he was about halfway to graduation. That summer Jackson returned to Virginia for the only extended period of leave he would get while a cadet. He could also boast that of the 78 cadets still in the class of 1846, he ranked 30th.

When he returned to West Point in August, Jackson learned that he had been appointed a sergeant in the corps of cadets. Undoubtedly, this appointment was made on the assumption that Jackson would continue to perform in an exemplary way in conduct. If so, it was a sound one. Jackson accumulated not a single demerit his entire third year at the academy. Moreover, while he continued to struggle in drawing, his overall performance in the January and June examinations was once again strong and kept him on track for finishing in the top half of the class. Surprisingly, though, given the skill at horsemanship that he had exhibited earlier in life, he struggled with cavalry training. "[T]hough accustomed to horse-back riding," one observer of his efforts in the riding hall later recalled, Jackson "was awkward, and when the order came to cross stirrups and trot, 'old Jack' struggled hard to keep his horse. When he advanced to riding at the heads, leaping the bars, etc., his *balance* was truly fearful, but he persevered . . . and certainly no one had our good wishes more than he."

Despite his solid performance during his third year at the academy, Jackson spent his final year at West Point as a "High Private." With the rest of his class, he found much of his last summer at the academy was dedicated to training in artillery. Like so much at the academy, the art of the artilleryman did not come easy to Jackson, but his grit and perseverance enabled him to get through the course of instruction.

When he and his classmates returned to the classroom in September 1845, they began the study of engineering under the tutelage of Denis Hart Mahan, whose class was in many ways the capstone course in the entire program at the military academy. In addition to being the unquestioned leader of the board of permanent professors who governed the academy's curriculum and operations, Mahan was by far its best-known and most influential instructor. His course, although devoted mostly to military engineering, was the only real instruction cadets received during their four years at West Point in the conduct of military operations, beyond the instruction and experience in managing small units they gained in the course of their day-to-day activities and summer encampments.

Jackson's performance in this class was solid, but unspectacular. In the January 1846 examinations he finished 41st in engineering but fourth in the ethics course. He would no doubt have scored higher had he not for some reason developed a profound concern around this time about his physical health, one that he endeavored to allay by taking long walks. He also adopted what appeared to his colleagues to be a number of odd habits, such as avoiding bending his body in order to ensure his internal organs could operate properly.

Nonetheless, he finished the program at West Point strongly. When the final grades came out for the 59 young men who completed the program in 1846, Jackson ranked a respectable 21st in military tactics and 24th in conduct. Considering he had started near the bottom of the class, these were remarkable achievements. Even more impressive was his finishing 11th in artillery and mineralogy, 12th in engineering, and 5th in ethics. Had the program continued another year, one observer was convinced Jackson—who only a few years earlier had been seriously contemplating how he would explain his failure to complete the course at West Point to his neighbors back in western Virginia— might well have risen to the top of his class. As it was, Jackson could not have been anything but satisfied in June 1846 when the final overall rankings were issued and he found himself 17th in rank.

As much as his achievement in rising so far during his four years was important in giving Jackson a well-deserved sense of personal satisfaction, it was also important from a practical standpoint. The degree of choice a West Point graduate had in terms of the branch he was assigned to after graduation was directly connected to his class rank. The top two graduates, Charles Stewart and George McClellan, were able to secure much-coveted appointments in the engineers. That was well beyond Jackson's hopes and, in any case, despite the struggles Jackson had experienced the previous summer, it was his decided preference to be assigned to an artillery unit. Fortunately, his rank was high enough to make this happen. To his immense gratification, Jackson learned during the summer of 1846 that he would begin his career as an officer in the U.S. Army as a member of the First Artillery Regiment. It was during a July trip to Jackson's Mill and Weston to see friends and family that Brevet Second Lieutenant Thomas J. Jackson learned of this welcome development. After a few days basking in the admiring attention of his former neighbors, orders reached Jackson on July 22 directing him to report to New York City.

When he reached New York, however, Jackson learned that most of the men and the guns of his unit, Company K, First Artillery, were en route to Texas. The unit's commander, Captain Francis Taylor, was still there, though, to confirm Jackson's appointment as company quarter-master. Jackson then spent about a week helping Taylor raise troops, collect horses, and make arrangements for forwarding them to the rest of the unit, during which he also signed the oath of allegiance before a justice of the peace, which officially marked the beginning of his service in the U.S. Army.

Finally, on August 19, Taylor and Jackson left New York. Both men, and the 30 new recruits accompanying them, undoubtedly felt a power-ful sense of excitement, for they knew they were not going to Texas to perform garrison duty. They were going to war.

Chapter 2

THE YOUNG LIEUTENANT

MEXICO

The war between the United States and Mexico, which would add millions of new acres of land to the United States and do much to sow the seeds of civil war, was over three months old when Jackson and Taylor left New York in August 1846. In May, when Jackson was still at West Point, an American army commanded by Brig. Gen. Zachary Taylor won two hard-fought engagements at Palo Alto and Resaca de la Palma. They were nowhere near decisive enough in their results, though, to persuade the Mexican government to concede defeat. Thus, the call was made for Capt. Taylor's "flying artillery"—so called because of the mobility their smaller guns provided—to be sent to the scene of operations ahead of its commander and the freshly minted lieutenant from West Point that had just been assigned to it.

After leaving New York, Taylor and Jackson did not tarry. They first made their way overland to Pittsburgh and from there traveled down the Ohio and Mississippi Rivers to New Orleans, where they caught up with most of the rest of Company K in September. They then proceeded by boat to Port Isabel, Texas, where they landed on September 22.

Although he lamented in a letter to his family from New Orleans that he as yet had no particular command assigned to him, Jackson was nonetheless eager to reach the front. Elements from Capt. Taylor's command that had been moved forward earlier had seen some action; however, the portion of Company K accompanied by Jackson and Taylor reached Texas too late to participate in the operations that produced the September 21–24 Battle of Monterrey, after which General Taylor agreed to an armistice in exchange for the surrender of the city.

Shortly thereafter, Capt. Taylor (who Jackson described in a September 1846 letter to a relative as "a Virginian and a very fine man") received orders to bring the portion of his command then with him to Carmargo, which was reached on October 5. After about a month battling insects and intense heat at Carmargo, Jackson's desire to move closer to the action was gratified when Taylor received orders to proceed to Monterrey. Upon reaching Monterrey on November 24, Company K was entirely together in one place for the first time since before Jackson's arrival in New York. For Jackson, this meant he had little to do, for all of the company's command slots were filled already, meaning his only job was to do whatever tasks Taylor needed from his quartermaster and be ready to fill in if something happened to one of the unit's other four lieutenants.

Five days after arriving at Monterrey, Jackson and his unit were once again on the move, this time toward Saltillo with the rest of General Taylor's army. It was hoped by American strategists that a move on Saltillo might provoke another major battle, and that if the Americans once again prevailed, it might induce the Mexicans to pursue peace. At the other end of the chain of command, Bvt. Lt. Jackson mainly hoped for an opportunity to see combat for the first time. The Mexicans, however, refused to oblige, and the Americans occupied Saltillo without firing a shot. Several weeks of desultory occupation duty followed for Jackson and the rest of Company K.

During that time, American plans underwent a monumental and fundamental change. Instead of continuing to push Taylor's operations in northern Mexico, which had clearly achieved about all they could, Washington decided to let Maj. Gen. Winfield Scott lead a campaign designed to seize the Mexican capital. Scott's command would land on the east coast of Mexico and capture the port town of Vera Cruz, then advance toward Mexico City following the National Road. To maximize

the prospects for success, it was decided that Scott would receive reinforcements from Taylor's command in the form of Brig. Gen. William J.
Worth's division, which included Company K, First Artillery.

Thus, on January 9, 1847, an undoubtedly delighted Jackson left
Saltillo to accompany his unit on a six-week journey to Lobos Island,
where Scott was assembling the forces he intended to lead against Vera
Cruz. Much to Jackson's chagrin, while making this journey, Mexican
forces commanded by Antonio Lopez de Santa Anna made an attempt
to destroy Taylor's army, which culminated in the February 23 Battle of
Buena Vista. Jackson could not conceal his disappointment at yet again
having missed an opportunity to see action. "It would have afforded
one much pleasure," he informed his sister Laura, "to have been with
the gallant and victorious General Taylor at the battle of Buena Vista
in which he has acquired laurels as imperishable as the history which
shall record the invasion of Mexico by our victorious armies." Then,
while awaiting transport to Lobos Island, Jackson found himself being
introduced by Capt. Taylor to Lt. Daniel Harvey Hill, a West Pointer
from South Carolina who had already seen combat. "He will make his
mark in this war." Taylor informed Hill, "at West Point; he came there
badly prepared, but was rising all the time, and if the course had been
four years longer he would have graduated at the head of his class. He
never gave up anything, and never passed over anything without understanding it." Hill and Jackson then took a short walk together on
a beach during which Jackson peppered Hill with questions about his
combat experiences. "I really envy you men who have been in action,"
he confided, "we who have just arrived look upon you as veterans. *I
should like to be in one battle.*"

Finally, on March 5, Jackson and the rest of the First Artillery arrived at Lobos Island. Four days later, the great assault on Vera Cruz
commenced and Jackson finally got his thirst for action satisfied. He was
part of the third wave of troops that landed unopposed on the beaches
just south of Vera Cruz. Once ashore, Scott almost immediately commenced siege operations against the town itself. In these, Jackson found
himself under fire for the first time as, despite not having formal command authority, he helped manage the guns of Taylor's command.
While doing so he attracted favorable attention for the cool competence
with which he supervised the firing of the guns, "as though he were on
dress parade at West Point," according to one witness, "in the midst of

a hurricane of bullets." By March 25, the defenders of Vera Cruz had had enough and opened surrender negotiations. Four days later they turned the town over to Scott's army. Although a bit nonplussed that Scott had allowed the town's defenders to withdraw instead of taking them prisoner, Jackson was nonetheless exultant at the victory and immensely satisfied with his role and conduct in what he proclaimed in a March 30 letter to his sister as an operation that "has thrown into our hands the strong hold of this republic and . . . in connection with other circumstances must in my opinion excel any military operations in the history of our country." As if this were not enough, he informed her, "My health is extremely good. I probably look better than I have in years."

Regardless of how Lt. Jackson felt, the health of the American army was a matter of grave concern to General Scott in the spring of 1847. A desire to avoid the dreaded "vomito"—yellow fever—which regularly swept through the region around Vera Cruz played no small role in his decision to put his command on the march toward Mexico City in early April. For this campaign, Jackson and the rest of Company K found themselves assigned to the division commanded by Brig. Gen. David Twiggs.

On April 8, Twiggs's division left Vera Cruz and four days later reached a strongly held Mexican position at Cerro Gordo. When Scott arrived on April 14 with the rest of his army, he quickly decided against a direct attack on the Mexican position. Instead, he would try to maneuver Twiggs's division into a position from which it could attack the enemy's left and rear. On April 18, Scott's stratagem worked to near perfection. Twiggs's attack completely routed the Mexican left and forced its commander, Santa Anna, to order a retreat. Although Jackson and his battery did not play a significant role in the battle itself, as the Mexicans began to flee the field Capt. Taylor received directions to participate in the pursuit of the enemy. While Taylor's efforts failed to add further laurels to the victory Scott and his army had magnificently won, Jackson's "great exertions" to ensure the caissons kept up with the guns received praise in Taylor's report on the battle.

The American army then occupied Jalapa for three weeks, during which Jackson learned that on March 3 the brevet had been dropped from his rank and he was now a full-fledged second lieutenant. He also took some spare moments to reflect on what he had learned from Scott and Taylor in a letter home, demonstrating that he had become a sharp observer of men and a keen judge of character. Scott, he proclaimed, was "by far the most talented and scientific and at the same time the most vain and conceited. His comprehensive mind embraces not only different objects and ends but their general and combined bearings. . . . If you call on him for a past time, he may disgust you . . . but if you call on him on business & military matters, then you may expect to call forth the mighty powers of his mighty mind, and upon information so obtained I would rather rely than on all the other officers in our army." While Taylor lacked Scott's intellect and was, Jackson believed, guilty of serious errors in his conduct of operations, which contrasted sharply with the skill that characterized the operations at Vera Cruz and Cerro Gordo, the young lieutenant nonetheless admired him as "a plain . . . straight-forward & undesiring man" who was "as brave as a lion."

While at Jalapa, Jackson also learned that his promotion to second lieutenant carried with it transfer from Company K in the First tJackson objected to the transfer, the latter due in part to reports that, because it was a heavy artillery unit, Winder's command was slated to remain at Jalapa when the army resumed the advance on Mexico City, but to no avail. Worse, the reports turned out to be true, and when the army departed from Jalapa shortly after Jackson reported to Winder on May 12, the young lieutenant had, he told his sister Laura 13 days later, "the mortification of being left to garrison the town of Jalapa." While her brother passed his time in Jalapa working on his Spanish and taking long walks, Laura gave birth to a son, which she named Thomas Jackson Arnold. Jackson responded by advising his sister that he had seen "many things of interest by the way of ornaments and fruits and wish that I had the opportunity of sending some to you and Thomas."

Much to Jackson's relief, he learned on June 18 that Winder had received orders to march his command to Scott's assistance. After a 90-mile march, which included a harrowing engagement with a band of Mexican guerrillas near La Hoya, Jackson and the rest of Company G caught up with Scott's army at Puebla on July 8. Shortly thereafter, Jackson learned that Scott had directed Capt. John B. Magruder to reorganize Company I of the First Artillery into a light unit of "flying artillery," and Magruder was looking for a second lieutenant. That Magruder's reputation as a company commander was not especially good deterred many talented artillery officers who might have otherwise jumped at the chance to join his unit, but not Jackson. His reasons for doing so were simple. "I wished to be near the enemy and in the fight," he later explained to a friend, "and when I heard John Magruder had got his battery, I bent all my energies to be with him, for I knew if there was any fighting to be done, Magruder would be 'on hand.'"

It turned out, though, that the army had another officer in mind for the post, Lt. Truman Seymour. This turned out to be to Jackson's good fortune. Seymour had not only been one of his classmates at West Point, but he despised Magruder and wanted nothing to do with him. Thus, he and Jackson were able to quickly and successfully appeal to higher-ups for a change in orders so they could switch assignments. On July 13, Jackson officially left Company G and reported for service with Capt. Magruder. He then spent over a month working with his new command while Scott completed his preparations for the final push against Mexico City.

For Jackson and Company I, which was attached to the division commanded by Brig. Gen. Gideon Pillow, the march out of Puebla began on August 10. A few days later, they emerged from the mountains and cast their eyes on the magnificent valley of Mexico. Yet, however much his men were thrilled by the scene before them, Scott faced a formidable problem. A Mexican army that was far superior to his in numbers was posted squarely between his own and Mexico City, with difficult terrain and a very limited road network complicating the task of operating against it. Nonetheless, aided by a talented group of West Point–trained engineer officers he surrounded himself with, Scott quickly developed a plan for solving the problem. He decided to swing around the Mexican position to reach a position from which he could approach Mexico City from the south, with the route traced by his engineers, most notably Capt. Robert E. Lee. Battles followed on August 19 and 20 at Contreras and Churubusco, which ended with the American army having achieved a decided advantage.

During the fighting on August 19, Magruder's battery and a battery of howitzers commanded by Lt. Franklin Callender received the task of following a party of 500 infantry as they worked to improve a rough road that Lee had identified as a route that could be used to flank the Mexican position. Around noon, however, Mexican heavy artillery caught wind of the American movement and began firing on them. Shortly thereafter, a young lieutenant on Pillow's staff and a former classmate of Jackson's at West Point named George B. McClellan arrived on the scene and reported that Pillow wanted Magruder's and Callender's batteries to move to a position only a thousand yards from the enemy.

By two in the afternoon, Jackson's section of two guns had taken up a position to the right of Callender's howitzers, while the other section of Magruder's was posted to their left. Unfortunately the position Pillow had selected for the two batteries was completely devoid of cover, and the 22 guns the Mexicans had on the scene were soon pouring a heavy fire on them. The lieutenant in charge of Magruder's other section went down with a mortal wound, but Jackson, demonstrating what one observer later declared to be his "indomitable sticking qualities," remained cool and calmly kept his men working their guns until darkness and rain brought an end to the battle.

Magruder could hardly have been pleased with the ordeal his command had been subjected to, which necessitated its being kept out of the fighting on August 20, which brought victory to American arms at Churubusco, and the orders that had put it in such a vulnerable position. ("Human stupidity can go no farther than this," was how one young officer later assessed Pillow's performance.) Of Jackson's conduct, though, Magruder had nothing but praise. "I cannot too highly commend him," he advised his superiors after the battle. That they agreed with his assessment of Jackson was evident in the fact that promotion to first lieutenant followed shortly thereafter.

A two-week lull in operations then ensued as Scott agreed to an armistice to give the man Washington had sent to negotiate a peace treaty an opportunity to do his work. When the effort proved fruitless, Scott resumed his offensive, targeting a group of buildings known as Molino del Rey. In a tough fight the Americans successfully assaulted the Mexican position at Molino del Rey on September 8, with Magruder's battery supporting their efforts, in part by repulsing a counterattack by Mexican cavalry. The following day, Jackson received directions from

Magruder to post his two guns in advance of the small hamlet of Piedad, which was forward of the rest of the army. Jackson did so promptly and soon found himself exchanging fire with the Mexicans in a brief artillery duel that produced considerable noise, but no casualties for Jackson's command.

Three days later, Scott targeted the last major obstacle standing between his army and Mexico City, the hilltop castle of Chapultepec. Dawn on September 12 found Jackson's section and the rest of Magruder's battery on the far left of Scott's line, pouring fire into the Mexican position as part of what would be a day-long bombardment designed to pave the way for a successful assault. The following morning, Jackson resumed the bombardment until around 8:00 A.M., when the artillery was ordered to back off to let the infantry do its work. The two regiments of infantry operating on the part of the field Magruder's command was posted, though, soon ran into trouble as their effort to advance on Chapultepec over a causeway encountered stiff resistance from Mexican artillery and infantry posted in a well-located redoubt in front of them.

Soon thereafter, orders reached Jackson directing him to advance and assist the infantry. Jackson obeyed with alacrity, pushing his two guns forward onto a road he later described as "swept with grape and canister, and at the same time thousands of muskets from the Castle pouring down like hail." Almost as soon as he reached the road, Jackson found himself in what he later described as "ticklish work," as all of his section's horses were hit and one of its guns was rendered immobile. His men soon began to panic and within a few moments began seeking whatever cover they could find.

Jackson, though, was a rock. He walked back and forth along the fire-swept road trying to reassure his men until a sergeant finally moved forward to help Jackson move the remaining gun into a decent firing position. This inspired another man to step forward to offer his assistance, but Jackson waved him off and told him to go to the rear to find infantry support. When later asked by a cadet at Virginia Military Institute (VMI) how he was able to stick with his command in such a difficult situation, Jackson replied, "If I had been ordered to run, I should have done so; but I was directed to hold my position, and I had no right to abandon it."

Soon thereafter, orders reached Jackson from division commander Brig. Gen. William Worth to pull back. Jackson refused and argued it would be more dangerous to do that than to remain where he was. Shortly thereafter, he saw Magruder riding toward him, only to have his horse shot out from under him. Magruder was unhurt and managed to reach Jackson, who persuaded him to see what he could do about getting the immobilized gun into action. Magruder did so, and soon Jackson's two guns were back in business and dueling with the much better placed Mexican guns, until Worth threw a brigade of infantry into the battle that was able to seize the Mexican redoubt.

By then, the entire Mexican position at Chapultepec was falling apart. Their commander ordered his defeated troops to try to rally at the gates of the capital. To prevent this from happening, General Scott ordered a vigorous push against the San Cosme gate. Still full of fight, Jackson tracked down some wagons to which he could attach his guns and rushed forward so fast that he soon found himself out ahead of most of the American army.

He was not the only one. Lieutenants Daniel Harvey Hill and Barnard Bee had also pushed their infantry hard, so hard in fact, that orders directing them to pull back a bit to link up with the rest of the American force did not reach them until they were a mile ahead of the rest of Scott's command. Jackson reached Hill and Bee with his two guns as their troops were driving the Mexicans along a causeway and were on the verge of ordering their men to pull back from their exposed position. Jackson immediately offered to support them. At that point Magruder arrived on the scene and, after a vigorous debate, set aside his own reservations and agreed to let the three lieutenants continue their advance.

Magruder's reservations about the wisdom of what Jackson, Hill, and Bee were doing were almost proven correct. After advancing a half-mile along the causeway, Jackson's, Hill's, and Bee's men caught sight of 1,500 Mexican cavalry charging toward them. Disaster was adverted when Jackson brought up his guns and opened a blistering fire on the tightly bunched Mexicans. Soon the Mexicans were in full retreat with Jackson, pushing his luck to the extreme, giving chase. "Whenever they got a little too far, we limbered up and pursued at full gallop until the bullets of their rear guns began to fall near the leaders," he later recalled, "then we would unlimber and pour it into them—then limber up again and pursue. We kept it up for about a mile. . . . It was splendid!"

That night, as Jackson contemplated a hole cut in his coat during the course of the day's fighting from a hill overlooking San Cosme gate, the Mexican army evacuated their capital. The next morning, after firing a few rounds to squelch a mob of civilians and give weight to Scott's threat to shell the city if it did not surrender by a certain time, Jackson joined the rest of the American army in triumphantly taking possession of Mexico City.

His justifiable pride in his performance was reinforced by what his superiors wrote about him in their reports. "If devotion, industry, tallent [sic] & gallantry are the highest qualities of a soldier," Magruder crowed, "then he is entitled to the distinction which their possession confers. . . . [W]hen circumstances placed him in command for a short time of an independent action, he proved himself eminently worthy of it." Pillow and Worth also singled out Jackson's performance for praise in their reports, as did Scott, who also made a point of personally complementing him during a reception shortly after the occupation of Mexico City. In formal recognition of his performance, he also received promotion to first lieutenant and brevet promotion to major.

The heady months of active and triumphant campaigning would be followed by months of tedious occupation duty while the American and Mexican governments haggled over the terms of a peace settlement. It was anything but arduous for Jackson. His quarters were in the national palace, the scenery was charming, and the food, especially fruit, which he developed a love for during this time, was both delicious and abundant. There were also plenty of pretty women but, although he joked in a letter to his sister about some day sharing his life with "some amiable Senorita," there is no evidence that Jackson took advantage of the significant spare time he had while in Mexico to develop a serious relationship with any.

In addition to improving his Spanish skills, much of Jackson's time during this period was taken up by a profound spiritual awakening. The primary agent in this appears to have been Capt. Taylor, who pushed Jackson to read and reflect on the Bible. Jackson did so and took advantage of an invitation to visit a monastery, which stimulated an interest in Catholicism that culminated in several meetings with the archbishop of Mexico. Although these contacts instilled in Jackson a respect for Catholicism, he ultimately decided it was not for him. Nonetheless, his dedication to study of scripture and developing his own spirituality continued to grow.

While Jackson pursued his newfound interest in religion, he also received exposure to some of the less salutary aspects of army life when he was asked by Magruder to serve as his second in a duel with Brig. Gen. Franklin Pierce. Fortunately, before he and Pierce could fight their duel, Magruder was forced to bow out for health reasons that also compelled him to temporarily give up command of the company in October 1847. (A second duel that Jackson was asked to serve as one of the seconds for did go off in early 1848. Fortunately, due in part to Jackson's interjection after the first round fired by both men did no damage, it ended with neither injured.) As senior officer, Jackson assumed command of Company I and carried out the duties of company command with his usual efficiency until December, when Lt. William H. French was transferred from another unit to be Magruder's replacement.

Jackson had no choice but to accept French's appointment, but relations between the two men would never be warm. Thus, it was on more than one count that Jackson was delighted in January to receive orders to return to Company K—although once again as its quartermaster. Two months later, to the immense relief of Jackson and just about every other member of the American army, who, despite the many charms occupation duty in Mexico offered, were eager to return home, the United States Senate ratified the Treaty of Guadalupe Hidalgo.

In May, the two countries officially ended the war by exchanging ratifications of the treaty, in which the United States secured ownership of about half of Mexico's territory. Out of this would eventually be carved the states of California, Nevada, Utah, New Mexico, and Colorado. The question of whether slavery would be allowed in this new territory had already become a major bone of contention, but that the nation as a consequence had moved a significant step along the road to a brutal civil war between the North and South would no doubt have struck the captain and first lieutenant from Virginia, first lieutenant from Vermont, and second lieutenant from Illinois who officered Company K as absurd. Foremost on their minds was their departure from Mexico City, which came on June 5.

This image of the future general, produced in the 1880s for the landmark series Battles and Leaders of the Civil War, *was based on a photograph taken of Jackson as a first lieutenant in 1848. (Johnson, Robert Underwood and Clarence Clough Buel, eds.,* Battles and Leaders of the Civil War. *New York: The Century Co., 1887.)*

After retracing their steps back to Vera Cruz, a little over a month later Jackson and the rest of the company boarded the *Mary Kingsland*, which reached New Orleans on July 17. Three days of basking in the cheers from the people of New Orleans followed, then a trip up the Mississippi River. The last leg of the trip was overland and formally ended on August 16 with the battery's arrival at Fort Columbus, New York, although shortly thereafter they were moved from that overcrowded post to Fort Hamilton.

PEACETIME DUTIES

Within a month after arriving at Fort Hamilton, Jackson managed to secure a three-month leave to visit his family in western Virginia. It was a bittersweet visit. He was happy to spend time with his sister and meet his namesake nephew, with whom he quickly developed a powerful bond. And there was an immensely gratifying reception the citizens of Weston arranged to celebrate the returning military hero, as well as what must have been a highly flattering offer from two of the community's leading lawyers to support him if he decided to study law with an eye on joining their practice.

However, the main upshot of the visit was to illustrate that a gulf had developed between Jackson and the community he had left over four years before. His increasing devotion to his Christian faith, for one, clearly clashed with his sister's growing disenchantment with religion. Moreover, his horizons had been too widely broadened, military life suited him too well, and the recognition his performance in Mexico had received both fired his ambitions and left him too abundantly confident of his prospects in his chosen profession for him to find much appeal in or comprehend those who desired the quiet, respectable peacetime life in western Virginia that was laid out before him. Indeed, he was confident enough of his professional prospects to tell the two attorneys who courted him, "If there is another war, I will soon be a general." But if he left the military or no war ever came, he lamented, "I will never be anything but Tom Jackson."

Thus, it was undoubtedly with some relief that Jackson departed western Virginia in November. After a short stop in Richmond en route, Jackson reached Fort Hamilton in mid-December and returned to duty. One of the first things that quickly impressed upon him that life in garrison in peacetime would be different from life on campaign was an order that had been issued by First Artillery commander Col. Ichabod B. Crane prohibiting mustaches. (Crane had first entered the service during the War of 1812, and during that conflict met Washington Irving, who would make his name famous in the 1820 short story *The Legend of Sleepy Hollow*.) Jackson complied with the order and, with his characteristic conscientiousness and self-discipline, plunged into his duties.

While tedious, Jackson's duties as company quartermaster were not especially burdensome, and like many officers he often found himself traveling to other posts on court-martial duty. Nonetheless, Jackson still found himself with plenty of free time while stationed at Fort Hamilton. This had the salutary effect of giving him time to study and further develop his religious interests, which Capt. Taylor continued to encourage. As it had in Mexico, Jackson's earnest desire to develop himself spiritually attracted the attention of local ministers. Perhaps the most important of these was Martin Philip Parks, a West Point graduate who had heeded the call to minister in the Episcopal Church, served as chaplain at the academy when Jackson was a cadet, and was serving as rector of a church in New York while also serving as chaplain at Fort Hamilton. In addition to encouraging and guiding Jackson's spiritual development, Parks also introduced him to Michael Scofield, the rector of a small church near Fort Hamilton. The combined efforts of Taylor, Parks, and Scofield led Jackson to embrace Episcopalianism, which was formalized by his baptism by Scofield into that church on April 29, 1849.

The great amount of free time Jackson had while posted at Fort Hamilton also, however, gave him time to turn his mind to less con-structive matters, such as the state of his health, which became a pre-occupation. Even the increased burdens that came with elevation to command of the Company K when Capt. Taylor went on a leave of absence in early 1849 were insufficient to turn Jackson's mind from a conviction that there was something seriously wrong with himself physically. He often complained in letters to his sister about problems with his vision, internal organs, joints, and just about every other part of his anatomy. These concerns prompted Jackson to consult frequently with doctors and experiment with a number of medicines and treat-ments. He also made a point of exercising regularly, adopting a strict regimen in regards to his diet, and reading voraciously about anatomy and physiology.

Jackson's time at Fort Hamilton came to an end in the fall of 1850 when he received orders to report for duty with Company E of the First Artillery, commanded by Capt. William H. French. Shortly thereafter, he learned this meant service in Florida, where he arrived in December 1850 after a brief trip to western Virginia to see his sister and her fam-ily. On December 18, after a two-day march through thick jungle, Jackson reached Fort Meade along with the other 52 men of French's command. Named for George Meade, the engineer officer who had se-lected its site and with whom Jackson would become quite familiar dur-ing the Civil War, Fort Meade was surrounded by swamps that served as breeding grounds for malaria during the summer and located next to the Peace River, along a military road that connected Fort Brooke on the Gulf of Mexico near modern Tampa with Fort Pierce on the Atlantic Ocean.

French was immediately dissatisfied with the location of Fort Meade and directed assistant quartermaster Jackson to chair a committee charged with investigating the possibility of relocating the post about a half mile to a higher piece of land. Jackson's group immediately endorsed French's idea, and by the end of 1850 the men of Company E were busy putting it into effect. French's punctiliousness and attention to detail initially served to foster a very positive relationship between him and Jackson, with French assigning the younger man important responsibilities and even going so far as to assist Jackson in his efforts to secure a captaincy in a new regiment.

However, Jackson quickly became unhappy with his situation in Florida. His duties, while important and challenging, were unstimulating. Moreover, the experience exacerbated a sense on Jackson's part that he was quickly approaching a professional dead end, which was clearly manifest in his effort to escape his situation by securing a captaincy and transfer to another regiment. Moreover, the harshness of Florida's climate further aroused Jackson's concerns about his health. As if this were not enough, his relationship with French deteriorated badly in 1851. The troubles began when French expressed dismay with the results of a scouting expedition Jackson led in late February. French subsequently began closely supervising his subordinate and interjecting himself into his work in a way that inevitably produced friction between the two men. By the end of March 1851, they were barely on speaking terms.

Thus, when Jackson learned that month that the Virginia Military Institute was looking to fill a professorship and his name had been suggested for the appointment, he immediately expressed interest. This development was to a large extent the work of Jackson's former comrade from the Mexican War, Daniel Harvey Hill. Hill had left the army shortly after the war to accept a teaching position at Washington College, which was located in Lexington, Virginia, right next to VMI. Since then, Hill had developed a good relationship with VMI's West Point-educated superintendent Francis H. Smith and made a point of bringing Jackson's name to Smith's attention when he learned of the vacant position. Further assisting Jackson's cause was John S. Carlile, who represented Jackson's home region in western Virginia in the state senate, was a distant relative, and served on VMI's Board of Visitors. With Carlile championing his candidacy, the Board decided on March 28 to formally offer the position to Jackson.

By the time a letter arrived notifying him of this development Jackson had had more than enough of Florida. His dispute with French had come to the attention of division headquarters, which during the first week of April unambiguously sided with French and rebuked Jackson. Shortly thereafter, Jackson called men from the command to his office in an effort to gather information about French's relationship with a servant girl, undoubtedly with an eye on using it against his commander. To his dismay, the men refused to cooperate. One of the noncommissioned officers then reported what was going on to French, who promptly placed Jackson under arrest. On April 13 Jackson responded by going over French's head to request release from arrest. He also advised their superiors that he had (as a matter of duty, of course) investigated whether French had been "guilty of conduct unbecoming an officer and gentlemen" and felt compelled to call for a formal Court of Inquiry to further pursue the matter.

In the days that followed, French defended his conduct in a message to headquarters and demanded prosecution of "the malevolent" Jackson for propagating "so malicious a slander and falsehood." For his part, Jackson pushed for an investigation not only of French's personal activities, but his entire tenure at Fort Meade. Fortunately for both men, department commander David Twiggs rejected both of their requests and directed them to drop the entire matter. Jackson agreed to do so. French, however, felt he had no choice but to pursue charges against Jackson.

Meanwhile, Jackson received Smith's note informing him of his appointment to teach at VMI and decided to accept it. On May 16 French authorized Jackson's release from arrest. Five days later, Jackson departed from Fort Meade on a furlough, which he had requested in order to visit his family in western Virginia and, he hoped, travel to Europe before reporting for duty at VMI. When Jackson arrived in Lexington in June for a visit, however, Smith asked him to forego his plans for a trip to Europe to ensure he would be on hand for the start of the academic year. Jackson agreed but did manage to find time that summer for a trip to New York in search of help for his dyspepsia.

After about a month and a half residing on the country farm of a doctor, in which his health greatly improved and he received extensive advice for maintaining it through diet and exercise, Jackson left New York and returned to Virginia eager to begin his duties at VMI. In light of the fact that he had no previous experience teaching, a friend asked Jackson whether he was anxious about the new turn he was taking in his professional life. "No," Jackson replied: "I expect to be able to study sufficiently in advance of my classes; for *one can always do what he wills to accomplish.*"

Chapter 3

TOM FOOL

VIRGINIA MILITARY INSTITUTE

The Virginia Military Institute (VMI) was almost exactly a dozen years old when Brevet Major Thomas J. Jackson reported for duty as a professor of natural and experimental philosophy and artillery tactics on August 13, 1851. At the time a new barracks was under construction, which meant the cadets not then on summer vacation were living in tents on the parade ground. Jackson also learned that the commandant of cadets was out of town, and that he was now the temporary commandant. Consequently, on just his second day at VMI he found himself supervising the cadets as they conducted parade and drill. Helping Jackson out was Thomas T. Munford, the senior cadet, who had given Jackson a copy of the school's regulations and described to him the typical schedule. Jackson welcomed and frankly acknowledged his need for Munford's help. "Adjutant," he remarked, "I am here amid new men, strange faces, other minds, companionless. I shall have to rely on you for much assistance until I can familiarize myself with the routine duties and the facilities for executing them." Nonetheless, Jackson also saw "a great similarity . . . to

West Point," which made him confident that he would soon "master all difficulties."

Munford found Jackson as good as his word. Each morning Jackson rose early and plunged into his new duties, leaving his lodging at the Lexington Hotel before sunrise and rarely returning until after night had fallen. He quickly impressed the cadets and his new associates with his emphasis on discipline and found he had a hard time containing his delight at the new assignment. "I am very much pleased with my situation," he informed his sister, "I have commenced my military duties and am reviewing one of my text books." His health, he added, was greatly improved, while his spirits were greatly bolstered by the fact that his second-story room at the hotel gave him "a lovely view of the mountain scenery."

In September, when the entire corps of cadets was once again on post, the new barracks were still not finished. Thus, Jackson received directions from the superintendent to lead the cadets on a practice march. He and the cadets left Lexington on September 9 and took a route that enabled them to visit a number of spas in the region, which gave Jackson an opportunity to try the waters, which he immensely enjoyed and which reinforced his satisfaction with his situation. "I am delighted with my duties," he wrote a relative from the resort spa at Warm Springs, "the place and the people." At the same time, he made clear that his professional conscientiousness had not dimmed in the slightest, declaring "I am anxious to devote myself to study until I shall become master of my profession."

By the time Jackson led the cadets back to Lexington on September 24, the barracks were finally completed and the academic year was ready to begin. Jackson then found himself sharing quarters with Maj. William Gilham, an 1840 graduate of West Point who had resumed his duties as commandant upon his return to Lexington. Like Jackson, Gilham had distinguished himself as an artillerist during the Mexican War. He also shared Jackson's devotion to discipline and possessed the ability to instill it into the cadets in a way that, one later wrote, "commanded our profound respect, admiration and love."

It quickly became evident, however, that for all Gilham and Jackson had in common, there existed a considerable gap in their abilities as instructors. Almost immediately, intense friction developed between the cadets and their new instructor of natural and experimental philosophy (what modern students know as physics). Jackson proved a demanding, rough-hewn, and exacting taskmaster, who had little sympathy for cadets who struggled academically. No one doubted his hard-earned knowledge of his subject (gleaned in desperate cram sessions prior to each lecture); however, it also quickly became clear that he lacked the innate ability necessary to make it interesting to his students. Instead, Jackson taught in a low-key, highly formal, strictly structured, and monotonous style in which he followed closely the material in assigned texts, while offering and tolerating little in the way of critical or creative thought. Moreover, the rigidity of his personality, dullness of his delivery, and lack of patience with cadets who lacked his own hard-minded discipline when it came to studies (which he saw as symptoms of personal weakness) grated on his students. Jackson, they complained, clearly failed "to realize that we are the sons of gentlemen" who did not appreciate being treated in what they perceived to be the manner in which officers treated "the common soldiers in the regular army."

It did not take long for the cadets to begin openly expressing an intense dislike for Jackson. They nicknamed him "Square Box" to mock his large feet, and "Tom Fool." "No one recalls a smile, a humorous speech, anything from him," a student later remarked, "He was simply a silent, unobtrusive man, doing his duty in an unentertaining way— merely an automaton. . . . He was not praised; he was abused." "Remarkably stiff and officially polite in his section room," another recalled, "He always mistered the cadets, and saluted them when they had completed their demonstrations at the blackboard, or he had finished questioning them." Even Col. Smith was forced to recognize that, "As a Professor of Natural and Experimental Philosophy, Major Jackson was not a success. . . . He was no *teacher*, and he lacked the tact required in getting along with his classes. . . . He was a brave man, a conscientious man, and a good man, but he was no professor."

Jackson was a bit more effective as an instructor of artillery. Certainly Smith, knowing of Jackson's reputation in the regular army and exploits in Mexico, entertained high hopes for him in this aspect of his job. Moreover, unlike the subjects he taught in the classroom, artillery was one for which Jackson had real enthusiasm. "As soon as the sound of the guns would fall upon his ears," one cadet later recalled, "a change would come over Major Jackson. He would grow more erect; the grasp upon his sabre would tighten; the quiet eyes would flash; the large nostrils would dilate, and the calm, grave face would glow."

If his work at VMI was of decidedly mixed quality, Jackson was nonetheless satisfied with his personal life in Lexington. The natural beauty of the region and its agricultural richness greatly appealed to Jackson, and he regularly took long horseback rides around Rockbridge County. His efforts to engage socially with the community were less effective due to his innate shyness and introspectiveness, as well as the rigid schedule he kept to protect his health. Although he conceded Jackson's health was not great, Daniel Harvey Hill later recalled that "he imagined that he had many more ailments than he really did have . . . these peculiarities attracted much attention, and he was much laughed at by the rude and coarse. But he bore all their jests with patience, and pursued his plan unmoved by their laughter. In like manner he carried out strictly the direction to go to bed at nine o'clock. If that hour caught him at a party, a lecture, a religious exercise, or any other place, he invariably left." Nonetheless, Jackson was able to quickly establish good, if not especially warm, relationships with fellow members of the faculty at VMI, while his friendship with Hill became particularly close.

Meanwhile, Jackson continued his pursuit of religious instruction. He sampled each of the four white churches in Lexington and, despite his earlier baptism as an Episcopalian in New York and the fact that Col. Smith and much of the VMI community worshiped at the Episcopal Church, soon began drifting away from that denomination and toward the local Presbyterian church. The fact that Lexington Presbyterian was the largest and most important church in the county probably played a role. More important, no doubt, was the fact that two men Jackson was especially close to during his first year in Lexington, Hill and local bookstore owner John B. Lyle, were both dedicated Presbyterians. Jackson also later recalled being attracted by "the simplicity of the Presbyterian form of worshiping and the preaching of her well-educated ministry." In November 1851, Jackson formally joined Lexington Presbyterian Church.

Jackson soon thereafter purchased a copy of the New Testament and began eagerly working through it. His faith ultimately became such an powerful force in his life that even Hill was struck by his friend's devotion, exclaiming, "I never knew any one whose reverence for Deity was so all pervading, and who felt so completely his entire dependence upon God." The strictness that already distinguished the way Jackson lived his life became even more pronounced. He prayed several times daily for guidance and to express appreciation for the Lord's blessings. "I have so fixed the habit in my own mind," he explained to a friend, "that I never raise a glass of water to my lips without lifting my heart to God in thanks and prayer for the water of life. Then, when we take our meals, there is the grace. Whenever I drop a letter in the post-office, I send a petition along with it for God's blessing upon its mission and the person to whom it is sent. When I break the seal of a letter just received, I stop to ask God to prepare me for its contents, and make it a messenger of good. When I go to my class-room and await the arrangement of the cadets in their places that is my time to intercede with God for them. And so in every act of the day I have made the practice habitual . . . almost as fixed as to breathe."

Jackson adopted the practices of tithing a tenth of his income to the church, reading the Bible and other religious tracts closely, and regularly attending prayer meetings. He also embraced Dr. William S. White, the pastor at Lexington Presbyterian, as a spiritual guide and father figure. By March 1852, Jackson found himself teaching in the church's Sunday school. Curiously, Jackson's devotion to his faith was never strong enough to prevent him from regularly sleeping during church services. "In spite of my resistance," he conceded to an associate when the matter came up, "I yield to my infirmity, then I accept as punishment the mortification I feel." After Jackson successfully resisted the efforts of a famous hypnotist who visited Lexington, the audience roared in laughter when a young lady exclaimed, "No one can put Major Jackson to sleep but the Rev. Dr. White!"

Thus, despite his troubles professionally, Jackson was satisfied enough with his life in Lexington that upon the expiration of his furlough, he decided to officially end his six-year career in the U.S. Army by resigning his commission on February 20, 1852. It would have been understandable if Jackson felt moments of regret over this decision in the months that followed, for his troubles with the cadets at VMI further escalated during that time.

In April, Jackson came into conflict with James Walker over the fourth-year cadet's handling of a problem Jackson had submitted for him to answer on the blackboard. After Walker failed on his third attempt to answer it to Jackson's satisfaction, the two began snapping at each other, which led Jackson to order Walker's arrest. When a court-martial on May 2 ruled in Jackson's favor, Walker responded by challenging him to a duel and threatened if "the professor failed to give him satisfaction in that way, he would kill him on sight."

Jackson would do no such thing, and his friend Hill supported his course throughout the entire episode. Nonetheless, the situation escalated to the point that Col. Smith decided to intercede. He went to court to get a restraining order against Walker and personally wrote to the expelled cadet's father asking him to come to Lexington and take his son home.

While Smith's actions effectively defused the situation involving Jackson and Walker, his relationship with Jackson was also troubled during this time. One afternoon during artillery drill, Smith felt compelled to verbally reprimand Jackson when the cadets under his command played a prank with one of the guns. An embarrassed Jackson responded by employing excessive formality in his dealings with Smith for weeks afterward.

As if this were not enough, in June one cadet's father felt compelled to write Smith to complain about what he described as Jackson's "rigid aversion towards him in his recitations." Despite Jackson's behavior following the incident involving the cannon, Smith wrote back to the father defending the young professor. Jackson, Smith explained, was in charge of a difficult department and was known to enforce regulations "with the most punctilious care." "When he is better known to the classes," Smith was certain, "he will be better liked, for they will discover that the highest toned principles actuate him."

After a summer break in which he took the waters at a nearby spa and spent time with family in western Virginia, Jackson began his second year at VMI with a new roommate and new quarters. Plus, he felt good physically, especially about his weight, which was six pounds heavier than ever before, something he interpreted as a very positive sign. He also joined a new county Bible society that fall, beginning what would be a very active six-year membership in the organization.

Undoubtedly the most positive development in Jackson's life during this time was his growing relationship with the family of Rev. George Junkin, the president of Washington College. In addition to further encouraging Jackson's zealous pursuit of spiritual development within the Presbyterian Church, it also enabled him to spend time with Elinor "Ellie" Junkin, the second of Junkin's daughters. By the end of 1852, with his efforts encouraged and facilitated by D.H. Hill and his wife, Jackson was actively courting Ellie. "I don't know what has changed me," he confided to Hill at one point, "I used to think her plain, but her face now seems to me all sweetness." "I burst out laughing," Hill later recalled, "and replied, 'You are in love; that's what is the matter!' He blushed up to the eyes, and said that he had never been in love in his life, but he certainly felt differently toward this lady from what he had ever felt before."

Ellie was receptive enough to Jackson's efforts enough to accept his proposal of marriage in early 1853. Unfortunately, her older sister Margaret (Maggie) did not approve of the match, and it was no doubt at her instigation that Ellie soon thereafter broke off the engagement. Jackson was devastated. "I don't think I ever saw anyone," his friend Hill later recalled, "suffer as much as he did during the two or three months of estrangement. He was excessively miserable, and said to me one day, 'I think it probable that I shall become a missionary, and die in a foreign land.'" As was his wont, Jackson sought comfort in his faith and, no doubt welcoming a diversion that would take his mind off the situation, decided to make a concerted effort to improve his skill at public speaking, which led to his joining a local literary society in March 1853.

Fortunately, Hill's wife stepped forward to try to patch things up between Jackson and Ellie. Due in part to her efforts, the engagement was soon back on, although Ellie insisted it be kept secret. Jackson's delight was evident, though, as he was much more actively engaged socially that spring and seemed more satisfied with his work as well. Finally, on August 4, 1853, to the surprise of just about everyone in the community and the great dismay of her sister, Jackson and Ellie were married. Dr. Junkin performed the ceremony.

After the service, Jackson and his new bride, accompanied by Ellie's sister Maggie, departed for a honeymoon that would take them to New

York and Canada. It included a trip to West Point, where Jackson later recalled the "beautiful plain, the frowning ruins of Fort Putnam, the majestic river, and magnificent scenery, all conspired to enhance my happiness which had already been of a high order." His travel companions likewise enjoyed the scene at West Point. They were less pleased shortly thereafter in Montreal when Jackson insisted on watching a local regiment drill and ran into some old West Point acquaintances. Jackson was so delighted that he ended up violating the Sabbath, which prompted complaints from his companions that he was "secularizing sacred time."

A visit to Quebec followed, where Jackson insisted on seeing the sites associated with the great 1759 British victory that wrested control of North America from the French. When they reached a memorial to British commander James Wolfe, Jackson's sister-in-law later remarked, Jackson removed "his cap, as if he were in the presence of some sacred shrine . . . his clear blue eye flashing with such a fiery light . . . his thin, sensitive nostrils quivering with emotion, and his lips parting with a rush of excited utterance, as he turned his face towards the setting sun, swept his arm with a passionate movement around the plain and exclaimed, quoting Wolfe's dying words—*I die content!*" "To die as *he* died," Jackson declared, "who would not die content!"

Although the trip did little to allay Maggie's dismay at her sister's marriage, upon their return to Lexington for the start of the academic year at VMI, Jackson and his wife quickly settled into a happy domesticity. They moved into a newly added wing of the Junkin home, and Jackson resumed the more active schedule of social engagements that his relationship with Ellie had undoubtedly inspired the previous year. He continued to participate in the literary society, taught Sunday school, was appointed to the board of directors of a local bank, and began taking a more active role in public affairs in Lexington. In early 1854, he was delighted to learn that his sister Laura, who was understandably a bit miffed at being kept out of her brother's marriage plans, had given birth to a daughter.

While cadets continued to find much to be desired in his teaching ability, over time Jackson's personal eccentricities became less obtrusive and, as his willingness to indulge their frequent requests to hear about them indicated, it was with no small delight that he learned word of his exploits in the Mexican War had aroused both their interest and admiration. As if this were not enough to satisfy Jackson, during the winter of 1853–54 he and his wife learned she was pregnant with their first child.

Nonetheless, the year was not without its challenges. Early in 1854, his mother-in-law died, while two of his sister's young children came down with serious illnesses, with one of them losing her battle. In both cases, Jackson drew strength from his continuing spirituality, although he was clearly troubled by reports that his sister was moving in an opposite direction in her relationship with God.

At the same time, Jackson was by no means unwilling to consider new opportunities. During his third year at VMI he made a serious effort to secure a professorship in mathematics at the University of Virginia. In addition to the prestige attached to such a position, Jackson's decision to pursue it was no doubt motivated in part by a desire to make his family more independent from the Junkins. Moreover, there was the fact that Col. Smith and Dr. Junkin, as the respective masters of two neighboring institutions, did not always get along, and in their conflicts Jackson found himself in the distinctly unpleasant position of being pulled in two directions. On top of this, his good friend Hill had grown disenchanted with life in Lexington and began seeking employment elsewhere, which ended with his securing a position at Davidson College in North Carolina. Yet, despite the fact that he collected an impressive list of references, Jackson's effort to leave Lexington for Charlottesville proved fruitless, as the position went to another man.

At the end of the 1853–54 academic year, Jackson and his wife decided to pay a visit to western Virginia. Although a physically rigorous trek, especially for Ellie, who was six months pregnant, the Jacksons managed to reach his sister's home in Beverly, where they had an immensely satisfying visit. Jackson's sister and wife got along very well, while Jackson was pleased to find his popularity with his sister's children was still strong and that they also took quite a shine to Ellie. Although the rigor of the travel to and from western Virginia left her exhausted when they returned to Lexington, it was with much optimism that Ellie and her husband anticipated the birth of their first child that fall.

On October 22, 1854, however, the hopes and joyful anticipation Jackson felt as his wife went into labor were abruptly—and cruelly—dashed. The child, a son, was delivered stillborn. Ellie at first appeared to be holding up well after the ordeal, well enough that the doctor felt he could leave Jackson alone with his wife. When Jackson entered the room, however, he immediately saw his wife was in extreme distress and called for the doctor's return. By the time he did so, Ellie was hemorrhaging so badly that the doctor was helpless to save her. Thus, in less than two hours, Jackson had to endure the loss of his child and his wife.

Jackson was crushed but suppressed his emotions, seeking solace in his faith. "I have been called to pass through the deep waters of affliction," he wrote his sister the day after, his words clearly reflecting the depth of his effort to work through the shock to cope and make sense of things. "The Lord giveth and the Lord taketh away, blessed be the name of the Lord," he declared, "as it is His holy will, I am perfectly reconciled to the sad bereavement, though I deeply mourn my loss. My Dearest Ellie breathed her last on Sunday evening, the same day on which the child was born dead. Oh! the consolation of religion! I can willingly submit to anything if God strengthens me. . . . I have joy in knowing that God withholds no good things from them that love & keep his commandments. And he will overrule this *Sad, Sad* bereavement."

Ellie Jackson and her child were laid to rest the next day in the town Presbyterian cemetery. It was a bitterly cold day, with snow falling, as a stoic Jackson watched the single coffin containing the remains of his wife and child be placed in the grave. One of the cadets from VMI who accompanied the coffin as it was escorted through town to the cemetery later wrote of Jackson that "He did not shed a tear, yet everyone who saw him was impressed with the intense agony he was enduring." Jackson was the last to leave the graveside, and he did not do so until Dr. White came back to personally escort him out of the cemetery. Jackson would return daily. Later he confided to D. H. Hill that more than once he had to fight the urge to dig up the coffin so he could "once more be near the ashes of one he had loved so well." "I look forward with delight to the day when I shall join *her*," he wrote his sister in November, adding, "Religion is all that I desire it to be. I am reconciled to my loss and have joy in hope of a future reunion."

Still, the months that followed were extremely rough for Jackson emotionally. The Junkin family naturally was supportive, and his bonds with them gained extra strength from the emotional pain that all felt. Margaret, who had so adamantly fought her sister's marriage to Jackson,

especially reached out to him, and the two developed a very close relationship during what was an unquestionably difficult period in both
of their lives. Still, Jackson continued to mourn, and if this were not
enough, he again began having health problems. A visit to western Virginia during the summer of 1855 did little to boost his spirits, but he
returned to Lexington determined to soldier through his personal grief.
Given that his primary source of solace was his faith, not surprisingly
Jackson threw himself into his church activities.

Perhaps the most notable of his endeavors during this time was his
effort to create a local Sunday school class for local African Americans.
Jackson had long deplored the lack of such a class in Lexington and,
despite some resistance from the local community, was successful in
setting one up. The class began in autumn 1855 with Jackson exercising the sort of tight control over its organization, curriculum, and per-
sonnel that characterized all of his activities. Before long he had over
80 students under his charge and earned not just the respect, but the
affection of many in Lexington's African American community. "In
their religious instruction he succeeded wonderfully," Dr. White later
wrote, "His discipline was systematic and firm, but very kind. . . . He was
emphatically the black man's friend."

In the course of his efforts, Jackson found his own faith strength-
ened, but this was not the only side benefit of this endeavor. His main
partner in it was John Preston, the assistant superintendent of the Presbyterian Church's Sunday school. Preston was one of Lexington's most
distinguished public men. A leading attorney and business man, he had
conceived the idea of creating a military college in Lexington, played
a central role in the effort to bring it to fruition with the creation of
VMI, and served on its faculty as a language professor. Due in part to
their mutual efforts with the Sunday school, Jackson and Preston became especially close, their bond receiving reinforcement in mutual
grief when Preston's wife of over 15 years died in January 1856.

When the academic year ended in 1856, Jackson attempted to leave
all of this temporarily behind. In June he received permission from
Col. Smith to take a leave of absence and headed to Europe. He traveled first to Great Britain, where he filled his waking hours sightseeing
and taking extensive notes on all he saw. He then crossed the English
Channel and did the same in Belgium, France, Germany, Switzerland,

and Italy. The breadth of his travels and the powerful impression of all that he saw were evident in his later warm recollection of "the romantic lakes and mountains of Scotland, the imposing abbeys and cathedrals of England; the Rhine, with its castellated banks and luxuriant vineyards; the sublime scenery of Switzerland, with her lofty Mont Blanc and massive Mer-de-Glace; the vestiges of Venetian beauty; the sculpture and paintings of Italy; the ruins of Rome; the beautiful Bay of Naples, illuminated by Vesuvius, and lovely France, with her gay capital."

In August Jackson returned to Lexington gushing with such enthusiasm over his trip that he felt compelled to warn one associate to never initiate a conversation on the topic unless he was prepared to endure a recitation of the "almost inexhaustible assemblage of proud and beautiful associations" he had picked up while oversees. He resumed teaching, although it quickly became clear that nothing had happened in Europe that translated to greater effectiveness in the classroom, and he remained a source of exasperation for the cadets. He also expanded his business interests and, perhaps having gained some fresh perspective on his earlier travails while in Europe, began looking for a new wife.

Jackson had grown especially close to Maggie Junkin in the time since her sister's death, but for them to have a romantic relationship would have violated Presbyterian canon, something that was unthinkable given the dedication to their faith that ironically made them so complementary. Fortunately, as they had before with Jackson, the Hills decided to take a hand in the situation. At the time D.H. Hill was serving as the head of the mathematics department at Davidson College in North Carolina. Davidson's president, Robert Morrison, had a daughter named Mary Anna, whom Jackson first met in Lexington shortly before his marriage to Ellie Junkin. Anna, according to a mutual acquaintance of hers and Jackson's, was "Fair in person, and beautiful in character—amiable and loving by nature—intelligent, cultivated, refined, and pious." As an added bonus, her elder sister Isabella just happened to be Mrs. Daniel H. Hill. Thus, there was undoubtedly more on the minds of all involved than simply seeing old friends that brought Jackson to the Hills' home in North Carolina in December 1856.

Jackson quickly won over the Morrison family to his efforts to court Anna. Indeed, he was so successful that by the time his visit was over the two were formally engaged. For the next few months, Jackson regularly wrote to Anna. He also clearly signaled his intentions by finally moving out of the Junkin home.

In July, Jackson once again left Lexington bound for North Carolina and on the 16th took 25-year-old Mary Anna Morrison as his wife. After a honeymoon trip that, as his first one had, took the Jacksons north to see West Point, Niagara Falls, and other sites in New York, they spent three weeks at Rockbridge Alum Springs to take the waters before reaching Lexington. There they made their residence at the Lexington Hotel on Main Street, where Jackson had been staying ever since moving out of Junkin home. That the relationship between Jackson and the Junkins remained unaffected by these developments was evident in the fact that probably no one worked harder than Margaret Junkin to help Jackson and his new wife negotiate Lexington society.

Jackson's personal life was complicated, however, by health problems. He suffered significant difficulties with his ears, and by 1858 an infection had significantly damaged his hearing in his right ear. He also battled chronic throat infections, as did his new wife (hers related to a serious thyroid problem), and neuralgia. Although he tried numerous medications in an attempt to fend off his illnesses, the most important source of comfort was, as always, his faith. He continued to attend church services every Sunday and direct the African American Bible school, while also managing to find time to teach Bible classes to young men. His devotion to his faith so impressed his fellow congregants that when elections were held in December 1857 to select deacons for Lexington Presbyterian Church, Jackson was one of three men who were unanimously elected to the office.

Jackson needed his faith in the late spring of 1858. On April 30, Anna gave birth to their first child, whom they named Mary Graham Jackson after her maternal grandmother. Jackson and his wife were delighted, but their joy quickly turned to sorrow. Within a few days it was clear that the child was not well. For three weeks, the Jacksons did what they could to help their baby fight off jaundice, but it proved a losing battle. On May 25, Mary died. A devastated Jackson once again buried his emotions as he arranged for his own family plot in Lexington's Presbyterian cemetery, where Mary Graham Jackson was laid to rest.

Shortly after the 1858 academic year ended, a still grieving Jackson and his wife traveled to New York City. While they spent some time shopping and sightseeing, the main purpose of the trip was to enable Jackson to see a doctor about his throat problems. In mid-August, he underwent surgery to remove an infection that was found on and around one of his tonsils, although it did not seem to associates when he returned to Lexington that the procedure had done much good.

For Jackson the 1858–59 academic year was in many ways a repeat of previous years. His teaching style had improved little, and the popularity of his class remained low among the cadets, although many possessed a healthy respect for his character and were accepting of his peculiarities. More vexing for Jackson that year was when he felt compelled by his problematic health to submit his resignation from the Sunday school and the office of deacon. (Also no doubt playing a role in Jackson's desire to relieve himself of some of his public responsibilities at this time was the fact that his nephew Thomas Jackson Arnold came to live with him and his wife in October and would stay with them for eight months.) In October 1858, though, the congregation, while willing to accept his resignation from the school, preferred to give him only a leave of absence as deacon.

An immensely gratifying aspect of Jackson's life during this period was the success he and his wife had in finding and establishing their first real home together. They purchased a house in Lexington, located on Washington Street only about a block from their church, in November 1858 and moved into it in January 1859, the same month Jackson celebrated his 35th birthday. There Jackson and his wife enjoyed a relationship whose warmth would have surprised those who knew him only publicly. "He luxuriated in the freedom and liberty of his home," Anna later declared, "and his buoyancy and joyousness of nature often ran into a playfulness and *abandon* that would have been incredible to those who saw him only when he put on his official dignity." Jackson referred to Anna as his "esposita" and "My Sunshine" and delighted in dancing with her. When not enjoying his wife's company, Jackson would read. Most of the volumes in his library were of history and biography, with many, not surprisingly, on military topics, although he also had an extensive collection of works on religion and the subjects he taught at VMI. Jackson also developed a love of gardening. To better pursue this, he acquired a tract of land just outside Lexington where he raised wheat and vegetables.

During this time the Jacksons also owned six slaves, evidence that although Jackson's relationships with African Americans and views on race—as was apparent in his efforts at the Sunday school—were more enlightened that many of his contemporaries, he fully accepted what southerners euphemistically called their "peculiar institution."

THE SECTIONAL CONFLICT

The fact that there was bitter disagreement in the nation about slavery and its future in the American republic was driven home with particular force in October 1859. Jackson had probably given little thought to this matter as he spent the summer of 1859 tending to his and his wife's health problems, which happily diminished sufficiently to enable him to resume his former work as church deacon and Sunday school teacher. Then, during the third week of October news reached Lexington of the radical abolitionist John Brown's failed attempt to provoke a slave uprising by seizing the federal arsenal at Harpers Ferry, located a little over 150 miles north of Lexington.

It hit Lexington like a thunderbolt. Many young men of military age in the area were seized with what one student at Washington College described as a "military fever." Like other communities throughout the South, Rockbridge County quickly organized a company of volunteer troops dedicated to defending its home against what white southerners in their overheated imaginations were certain to be a wave of abolitionist raids to come.

Virginia governor Henry Wise, under whose authority Brown was quickly tried for treason and sentenced to be hanged, deemed it necessary that the cadets of VMI be on hand to ensure Brown's sentence would be carried out without mishap. At 10:00 P.M., on November 25, Jackson departed Lexington along with the cadets and other members of the faculty, all of whom Col. Smith placed under the overall command of Maj. Gilham. Jackson was in charge of the two pieces of artillery that were selected to travel to Charlestown to attend Brown's execution. Upon their arrival two days later, Jackson found, he told his wife, "about one thousand troops here, and everything is quiet so far. We don't expect any trouble. . . . I am much more pleased than I expected to be; the people appear to be very kind."

On December 2, 1859, with Jackson and his two guns less than 50 yards from the scaffold, Jackson watched as Brown arrived on the site at around 11:00 A.M. "He behaved with unflinching firmness," Jackson informed his wife, "He was dressed in carpet slippers of predominating red, white socks, black pants, black frock coat, black vest & black slouch hat. Nothing around his neck besides his shirt collar. The open wagon in which he rode was strongly guarded on all sides. . . . I was much impressed with the thought that before me stood a man, in the full vigor of health, who must in a few minutes be in eternity. I sent up a petition that he might be saved. Awful was the thought that he might in a few moments receive the sentence 'Depart ye wicked into everlasting fire.' I hope that he was prepared to die, but I am very doubtful."

When Brown reached the scaffold "with apparent cheerfulness," the final preparations were made. Then, Jackson wrote, "the rope was cut with a single blow, & Brown fell through about 25 inches, so as to bring his knees on a level with the position occupied by his feet before the rope was cut. With the fall his arms below the elbow flew up, hands clenched, & his arms gradually fell by spasmodic motions—there was very little motion of his person for several minutes, after which the wind blew his lifeless body to & fro."

Four days later, Jackson and the rest of Gilham's command boarded trains at Harpers Ferry and traveled to Richmond. They did so at the request of Governor Wise, who wished to review the cadets. On December 8, the review took place, with one observer expressing admiration for all but "Commandant of the battery." Jackson, he declared, was the only part of "this fine body that struck me as in any way lacking in soldierly appearance"—though he did concede Jackson appeared "to be deeply intent on his business."

By the time he returned to Lexington from his adventure, Jackson had contracted a cold. Yet he seemed immune to the sense of anxiety that still prevailed in his community as a consequence of Brown's actions. He did not share the fear that they were part of a larger conspiracy to flood the South with abolitionists seeking to stir up slave rebellions. Rather, Jackson's focus remained on his own situation. He fretted over his wife's and his own health, maintained his active involvement in the Lexington community, and tended to the home, gardens, and fields that gave him such delight.

With tensions gripping the nation as a whole as it headed into what would be a tumultuous presidential election year in January 1860, Jackson conceded to a relative in a letter that, "Viewing things from Washington from human appearance, I think we have great reason for alarm." Yet, as he always did, he found reassurance in the thought that a higher and wiser power was at work. "[M]y trust is in God," he declared, "and I cannot think he will permit the madness of men to interfere so materially with the Christian labors of this country."

Shortly after the 1859–60 academic year ended at VMI, Jackson and his wife were sufficiently untroubled by the brewing crisis between the North and South to travel to Vermont and Massachusetts in search of relief from their physical ailments at some highly recommended medicinal spas. The treatments had a decidedly salutary effect on Jackson and his wife, and they both sought to extend their time in New England in order to complete the regimen of treatments they started that summer. Jackson's petition to postpone his return to VMI was denied; however, they agreed that Anna would stay to continue receiving treatment.

It was undoubtedly with a heavy heart that Jackson returned alone to Lexington. He found the entire community concerned about the 1860 presidential election and the possibility that it might be the catalyst for a disruption of the Union. Jackson favored the Union and questioned the wisdom of secession, while also believing that the individual states had rights that should be respected and that secession was a legitimate—if undesirable—means for protecting them. While uncomfortable with the emotionalism and wild talk the presidential contest was stimulating, Jackson nonetheless decided to attend a rally for John C. Breckinridge. Breckinridge was the candidate of the southern faction of the Democratic Party that had broken away from the rest of the party over the majority northern faction's unwillingness to support a federal slave code for the territories. At the rally, Jackson spoke briefly to express his support for Breckinridge, but beyond this, his main preoccupations that fall were the absence of his wife and his duties at VMI.

To the surprise of few in Rockbridge County, or anywhere else in the country for that matter, Republican candidate Abraham Lincoln won the November election. Not a single vote was cast for him in Rockbridge. Jackson nonetheless remained hopeful that divine Providence would prevent this event from being the catalyst for a rendering of the Union and civil war, but these hopes were to be dashed. On December 20, South Carolina left the Union, and by mid-February 1861 six other states had followed.

Jackson hoped for peace. He resolved to vote for candidates who opposed secession to the convention the Virginia legislature had called to consider the state's relationship with the Union, that is, unless it appeared the Lincoln administration and the people of the free states were not willing to respect Southern rights. Among these rights, Jackson recognized, the ownership of slaves enjoyed a special place of privilege.

"People who are anxious for war don't know what they are bargaining for; they don't see all the horrors that must accompany such an event," Jackson advised his nephew and namesake in January. He was glad that at that time support for the Union seemed the prevailing sentiment in Virginia. Jackson proclaimed himself, "in favor of making a thorough trial for peace. . . . I desire to see the state use every influence she may possess in order to procure an honorable adjustment of our troubles. . . . For myself I have never yet been induced to believe that Virginia will ever have to leave the Union. I feel pretty well satisfied that the Northern peoples love the Union more than they do their peculiar notions of slavery."

At the same time, he told his nephew that he believed that if the effort to preserve the peace failed and Virginia was invaded, such an invasion must be met "with terrific resistance—even to taking no prisoners." If, he declared, "free states instead of permitting us to enjoy the rights guaranteed to us, by the Constitution . . . should endeavor to subjugate us, and thus excite our slaves to servile insurrection in which our Families will be murdered without quarter . . . it becomes us to wage such a war as will bring hostilities to a speedy close."

Jackson provided a vivid illustration of his opposition to secession in late February 1861. When he arrived on the parade ground to participate in the annual salute to George Washington's birthday, to his great dismay Jackson was greeted with a decidedly unwelcome sight. Instead of the flag of the United States, a hastily prepared secession flag proclaiming "Hurrah for South Carolina" was flying above the barracks. He immediately ordered it removed and the U.S. flag returned to its previous place of honor.

But Jackson was resisting a tide that ultimately became all but unstoppable. Word arrived in mid-April that troops serving the government secessionists had organized in Montgomery, Alabama, to govern the newly proclaimed Confederate States of America had fired on a Union fort in Charleston Harbor. In the aftermath of this event, the crisis quickly moved to a point of no return.

In response to the Lincoln administration's call for 75,000 troops to put down "combinations too powerful to be suppressed by the ordinary course of judicial proceedings" the Virginia convention decided to cast the Old Dominion's lot with the Confederacy. In a remarkable swing in sentiment, Rockbridge County went from a relatively evenly divided, but Union-leaning community, to one that was solid in its support for secession. One of the few holdouts was the president of Washington College. Dr. Junkin's brave stand against secession and refusal to relent one bit in his love for the Union almost overnight transformed him into a pariah. Heartbroken, he resigned his post and relocated to Pennsylvania, where he became a passionate Republican.

While this drama played out at Washington College, VMI became a veritable beehive of activity. Few doubted that secession would mean war and that the young men, past and present, who had passed through the program at the institute would have a significant role to play in Virginia's war effort. On Sunday, April 21, Jackson learned that the state's governor, John Letcher, wanted the 176 cadets to come to Richmond to serve as drillmasters and that Jackson had been selected to lead them there. After a few hours overseeing preparations at the institute, eating breakfast, finishing his paperwork, packing, and praying with his wife for guidance and protection on his new endeavor, at 12:30 p.m., Jackson mounted his horse and began leading his charges out of Lexington.

One man who accompanied Jackson that day later recalled that the major "was eager for vigorous operations without delay. He was full of fire and eagerness. He cast his eye repeatedly along the artillery column . . . and alluded to his marches in Mexico which the present scene brought back to his memory." That evening, Jackson and the cadets reached Staunton. There they spent the following morning boarding the trains of the Virginia Central Railroad that were to take them to Richmond.

Chapter 4

STONEWALL

JACKSON TAKES COMMAND

When Jackson arrived in Richmond on April 22, 1861, he learned that Robert E. Lee, a fellow veteran of Winfield Scott's campaign against Mexico City, had been appointed major general and commander of Virginia's military forces. It was, in his mind, a most welcome development. "This I regard as of more value to us than Gen. Scott could render as Commander," he proclaimed in a letter to his wife, "I regard him as a better officer than Gen. Scott." Lee was not the only one winning praise from those watching Virginia authorities prepare for war. "Jackson is truly a benefactor," one man in Richmond proclaimed shortly after his arrival from Lexington, "I hope he will take the field himself . . . if he does I predict for him a successful career."

Upon reaching Capitol Square, Jackson and the VMI cadets were reviewed by Governor Letcher. They were then ordered to Camp Lee, which had been named for Gen. Lee's father, the famed Revolutionary War cavalry commander Henry "Light Horse Harry" Lee. Although he had no instructions regarding what was expected of him after he turned over the cadets to the state, Jackson decided to say in Richmond and offer his services as a drillmaster. He and 12 of the cadets who accompanied him soon thereafter found themselves directing basic artillery drills under the supervision of the same John Magruder who had commanded him in Mexico.

Then, on April 25, Jackson learned he had been appointed to the topographical engineers as a major. While the topographical engineers had commanded greater prestige than the artillery in the antebellum army, Jackson recognized that in wartime a combat branch assignment was far more desirable and was displeased at this development. However, much to Jackson's relief, the following day Governor Letcher decided to appoint him a colonel. The appointment was made official the following day, with one of Jackson's associates from western Virginia appealing to the council that advised the governor on military appointments to give him even greater responsibility. "Maj. Thomas J. Jackson is," he declared, "by all odds the best man we can procure for chief command in Northwestern Virginia."

That same day, Jackson received directions to report to the governor's mansion. There Letcher informed him that it he was to command Virginia troops then assembling at Harpers Ferry. As he prepared to leave Richmond that evening, Jackson received orders from Lee confirming that he was to "proceed without delay to Harpers Ferry . . . and assume command of that Post." "After mustering into the service of the state such Companies as may be accepted under your instructions," Lee instructed, "you will organize them into Regiments or Battalions."

Travel to Harpers Ferry gave Jackson an opportunity to experience first-hand the transportation network on which much of Virginia's military effort would have to rely. He first traveled west to Gordonsville on the Virginia Central Railroad, then northeast to Manassas Junction on the Orange and Alexandria Railroad, then west again on the Manassas Gap Railroad to Strasburg. After a 20-mile ride on horseback from that place to reach Winchester, he spent the evening there before making the last leg of his trip on a Winchester and Potomac Railroad train bound for Harpers Ferry.

Upon arriving at Harpers Ferry on April 29, Jackson found the approximately 2,500–3,000 men there operating under the command of Kenton Harper. Harper had learned to his dismay two days earlier that his rank as a major general in the state militia, and those of the three brigadier generals then at Harpers Ferry, would be rendered null and void upon Jackson's arrival from Richmond. To his own dismay, Jackson found these officers, while finely uniformed and accompanied by large staffs, had accomplished little in the way of organizing or training the troops that had gathered at Harpers Ferry in the weeks since Virginia militia had compelled federal authorities to evacuate the town on April 18. Thus, it was no doubt with considerable mutual relief that Jackson also discovered a number of VMI cadets were at Harpers Ferry as well. "I am glad to see you," he advised them, "and will take special interest in you." Far less impressed was a newspaper correspondent. After watching Jackson go about his business wearing a plain blue uniform and focused demeanor that contrasted sharply with those who had previously exercised command at Harpers Ferry, the correspondent declared, "The Old Dominion must be sadly deficient in military men, if this is the best she can do. He is nothing like a commanding officer. There is a painful want in him of the pride, pomp and circumstance of glorious war."

Jackson immediately went to work. A rigorous program of drill and instruction, with a cadre of VMI men leading, was instituted. The chaos and holiday atmosphere that greeted Jackson on his arrival quickly gave way to one in which order and discipline were the order of the day. Jackson made clear that he accepted that mistakes would be made in the process of learning the way of the soldier and went out of his way to be courteous to those under his command. At the same time, he also made clear that there would be no tolerance of negligence or inattention on the part of officers and enlisted men.

As he tended to the organization and discipline of his command, Jackson also spent a considerable amount of time thinking about his tactical and operational situation. He gathered information about the region by regularly riding about the countryside. He did so riding a horse that had been seized from a livestock train by an enterprising band of soldiers under the direction of quartermaster officer Major John Harman of Jackson's staff. When Harman presented Jackson with the fruits of this little operation, which consisted of four cars of cattle and one of horses, Jackson decided to purchase two of the horses: one large gelding for himself and a small sorrel gelding for Anna. However, he soon found that the softer gait and incredible endurance the latter possessed was better suited to his needs and quickly it became his main mount. Although he had named it Fancy, it quickly became better known as Little Sorrel.

The fact that Harpers Ferry was a significant industrial town, located at the northern end of the rich Shenandoah Valley, and one of the nation's great hubs in terms of water and rail transportation, made the town of obvious strategic importance to both the North and South. However, the topography of the region made it indefensible without possession of the high ground that surrounded the triangle of land where the Shenandoah River flowed into the Potomac River, on which the town was located.

While Loudoun Heights on the other side of the Shenandoah and Bolivar Heights behind the town were both important, it was Maryland Heights, located on the Maryland side of the Potomac opposite Harpers Ferry, that was most critical to the town's defense. Thus, within a week of assuming command, Jackson posted forces there and decided to fortify the heights. Then, on May 6, he sent a message to Lee in Richmond reporting that, aside from a few scattered detachments, he had mustered all of the troops then at Harpers Ferry into the service. "There are four 6-pounder guns here without caissons," he noted and asked Richmond to send any it might be able to spare, as well as a good engineer officer, "and also two 6-pounder batteries and two extra 12-pounder howitzers, all fully supplied with ammunition, horses, equipments, and everything necessary for being turned over to companies now waiting for them."

He also notified Lee that around two-thirds of the machinery from Harpers Ferry's musket factory had already been removed from the town and was en route to Winchester. Reports indicated the Federals had about four thousand troops in the vicinity of Chambersburg, Pennsylvania, and, Jackson assured Lee that if they "advance in this direction, I shall no longer stand on ceremony." "I have occupied the Virginia and Maryland Heights," he added, "and I am about fortifying the former with block-houses of sufficient strength to resist an attempt to carry them by storm. Whenever the emergency calls for it, I shall construct similar works on the Maryland Heights."

While Jackson's keen interest in the occupation of Maryland Heights was tactically sound, there was the serious strategic problem

A recent photo of the confluence of the Shenandoah and Potomac Rivers at Harpers Ferry. The view is from Maryland Heights, which figured prominently in Jackson's operations in the region in both 1861 and 1862, and offers a good sense of just how critical this point was to the town's defense. (Richard Gunion/ Dreamstime.com)

that Maryland had not yet seceded from the Union, though there were hopes that it would. It was a very delicate situation politically that made it essential that the greatest caution be taken in executing any course of action that might offend or antagonize the state's residents. Indeed, when Jackson informed Lee on May 6 that he had placed a small force on Maryland Heights—launching in effect the first Confederate invasion of the North—he explained that he had not yet fortified his positions there "by a desire to avoid giving offense" to the state.

Nonetheless, after a reconnaissance of Maryland Heights the following day, Jackson concluded he could not wait and advised Lee that he had to "fortify them at once, and hold them, as well as the Virginia Heights and the town, be the cost what it may." Jackson then once again urged Lee to send him more arms and disciplined troops. He suggested the posting of two pieces of artillery on Loudoun Heights and "a large number of 6-pounders on the Maryland Heights. Heavier ordnance, in addition to the field pieces referred to in yesterday's letter could be advantageously employed in defending the town." He then advised Lee that "I would be more than gratified could you spare the time for a short visit here, to give me the benefit of your wisdom and experience in laying out the different works, especially those on the heights. I am of the opinion that this place should be defended with the spirit which actuated the defenders of Thermopylae, and, if left to myself, such is my determination. The fall of this place would, I fear, result in the loss of the northwestern part of the State, and who can estimate the moral power thus gained to the enemy and lost to ourselves?"

Although he understood Jackson's perspective on the matter, having personally seen the terrain around Harpers Ferry while commanding the force that captured John Brown in 1859, Lee disagreed with Jackson's decision to occupy and fortify Maryland Heights. Thus, three days after Jackson's letter of May 6 arrived, Lee wrote back to express gratification "at the progress you have made in the organization of your command," but also indicated that the occupation of Maryland Heights was not approved by Richmond. "In your preparation for the defense of your position," Lee advised, "it is considered advisable not to intrude upon the soil of Maryland, unless compelled by the necessities of war." Jackson immediately wrote back to report that he had been informed that the Federals had four thousand troops about 50 miles away at Chambersburg, Pennsylvania, and explain that he had only put 500 men on Maryland Heights. Lee replied the following day that, "I fear you may have been premature in occupying the heights of Maryland with so strong a force near you. The true policy is to act on the defensive, and not invite an attack. If not too late, you might withdraw until the proper time."

While Jackson's focus during this time was on his professional duties, he could not block out personal issues that arose as a consequence of recent events. His sister Laura, Jackson learned, did not share his belief, which he expressed to a friend who visited him at Harpers Ferry, that, "As a Christian man, my first allegiance is to my State, the State of Virginia; and every other State has a primal claim to the fealty of her citizens." Instead, in asserting her loyalty to the Union, she followed the path of many of her neighbors, whose opposition to secession was rooted in economic differences with the rest of Virginia, their much lesser dependence on slave labor, and longstanding resentments against the eastern section of the state.

The fact that Unionism was strong in northwestern Virginia also posed a potentially serious threat to Jackson's left flank. He was more concerned, though, during the first half of May with the menace Federal troops concentrating at Chambersburg might pose to what he perceived to be an exceedingly exposed position at Harpers Ferry. Before anything could come of this, however, on May 15 the region ceased to be Jackson's responsibility. That day the Confederate War Department, which had taken over direction of the war upon Virginia's formally joining the Confederacy, decided to instead assign command of Harpers Ferry to Brig. Gen. Joseph E. Johnston.

Jackson did not learn of this development until Johnston suddenly appeared at his headquarters during the afternoon of May 23. Although hardly enthusiastic at this development, upon seeing written documentation for Johnston's appointment, Jackson accepted it. Whatever wounded pride Jackson may have felt at being superseded was undoubtedly somewhat alleviated when, four days after his arrival, Johnston decided to combine all of the regiments of Virginia troops that had been mustered into service at Harpers Ferry into a single command with Jackson as their commander.

This unit, the First Virginia Brigade, initially consisted of four regiments, all of which had been raised in the Shenandoah Valley, with the 4th and 27th Virginia coming from communities located at the southern end of the Valley, such as Lexington, Wytheville, and Pulaski. The 5th Virginia was raised largely from Augusta County in the middle of the Valley, while the ranks of the 2nd Virginia were filled by men from communities north of Staunton, such as Harrisonburg and Charlestown. (In July a fifth regiment, the 33rd Virginia, whose ranks were also drawn from the communities north of Staunton, would be added to the brigade.) Also attached to Jackson's command was the Rockbridge Artillery. Commanded by William N. Pendleton, the rector of Lexington's Episcopal Church, the unit had four guns, which had been named Matthew, Mark, Luke, and John.

With Johnston picking up the duties and responsibilities associated with overall command, Jackson focused his energies on training and instilling discipline in his brigade. As he did so, Johnston was coming to a different solution to the problem of defending Harpers Ferry than the one Jackson had reached while in command. Recognizing as did Jackson that the town was indefensible without control of the surrounding high ground and, no doubt having the desire to avoid provoking Maryland strongly impressed upon him by the authorities in Richmond before he departed to take command, Johnston instead requested authority from Lee to abandon Harpers Ferry. "I regard Harper's Ferry as untenable by us against a strong enemy," he later remarked. "We were bound to a fixed point; his movements were unrestricted."

Finally, on June 13, Richmond granted Johnston authorization to evacuate Harpers Ferry and move south up the Shenandoah Valley toward Winchester. The following morning, with Jackson's command tasked with ensuring that everything of value in the town was removed or destroyed, the Confederates left Harpers Ferry. Jackson and his men carried out their work enthusiastically, destroying the railroad bridge and thoroughly torching the town. Upon reaching Bunker Hill just north of Winchester, Johnston halted his command and, after posting them in a good defensive position, proceeded to formally organize the 9,000 men under his command in the region into an "Army of the Shenandoah" of four brigades.

Shortly after arriving at Bunker Hill, Johnston directed Jackson to take his brigade north to Martinsburg. There it would link up with a force of about 300 cavalry commanded by Col. James E. B. Stuart, then destroy the railroad yards located at Martinsburg to render them unusable to the enemy. Jackson's men set out on June 19 and upon reaching Martinsburg went to work with a thoroughness and zeal that was truly impressive. They had just about finished their work in Martinsburg when a report arrived of a Union force approaching the town. Jackson immediately forwarded the news to Johnston and excitedly prepared his forces to meet the enemy. Johnston immediately threw cold water on Jackson's efforts. He informed his eager and combative brigade commander that he was to avoid an engagement with the enemy at that time.

Jackson promptly complied with his superior's wishes and moved his command out of Martinsburg to a camp a few miles north of the town. At what became known as Camp Stephens, the brigade spent the next two weeks drilling and training, with their commander imposing a level of discipline that inspired one officer to declare Jackson was "considered rigid to the borders of tyranny by the men here."

An opportunity to test the men in combat finally came on July 2. Early that morning a report from Stuart reached Jackson that stated a Federal force had crossed the Potomac River and reached a point about five miles from his camp. Despite admonitions from Johnston to avoid anything that might bring about a serious engagement with the enemy, Jackson immediately put his command on the march toward Falling Waters on the Potomac.

Before he could reach Falling Waters, Jackson, riding at the head of his command, caught sight of Union cavalry. He directed Pendleton to deploy three of his guns and led the fourth forward along with his infantry. As Jackson's men advanced, Union artillery opened fire. Two regiments of Federal infantry then arrived on the scene and pushed Jackson's advanced force back. Jackson directed Pendleton to prepare his gun for action, and Pendleton finished doing so just as a force of Federal cavalry approached along the road from Falling Waters. A few rounds from Pendleton's gun effectively halted their advance, but, recognizing he was outnumbered, Jackson decided to pull back, in line with Johnston's earlier admonition to withdraw if faced with a strong enemy force.

Aided by Stuart's cavalry, Jackson did so successfully and had his men back at Camp Stephens by noon. Shortly thereafter, a far superior Federal force appeared on the scene and threatened to overlap both flanks of a line Jackson's command had hastily established. Thus, he ordered his men to abandon Camp Stephens and fall back south to Darkesville, where they were joined the following morning by Johnston and the bulk of the Army of the Shenandoah. Johnston's arrival was sufficient to make the Federals content with simply possessing Camp Stephens. On July 8, Johnston ordered his command back to Winchester.

Johnston praised Jackson's performance at Falling Waters and the effectiveness of his efforts in training his men that were evident in the short engagement. He advised Richmond to promote both Jackson and Stuart. Authorities in the capital, though, had already decided such a move was in order. On July 3, Robert E. Lee wrote to Jackson to inform him that it had been decided to commission him a brigadier general in the Confederate Army.

"My promotion is beyond what I anticipated," Jackson wrote to his wife from Winchester. "One of my greatest desires for advancement is the gratification it will give my darling & of serving my country more efficiently." Shortly after returning to Winchester, Jackson's authority was further expanded by the addition of another regiment, the 33rd Virginia, to his brigade. "Look how kind our Heavenly Father has prospered us," an evidently satisfied Jackson wrote his wife on July 16, "I feel well assured that in following our rule, which is Biblical, I am in the path of duty, & that no evil can come."

STONEWALL

The same day Jackson penned these words of comfort to his wife, Brig. Gen. Irvin McDowell commenced major operations in northeast Virginia by marching an army of about 30,000 Federal troops out of Washington. McDowell's objective was Manassas Junction, where the railroad running south and west out of Alexandria, Virginia, connected with a railroad that linked Confederate forces commanded by Brig. Gen. Pierre G. T. Beauregard in northern Virginia with Johnston's forces in the Shenandoah Valley. When news of McDowell's advance reached Richmond, Confederate military authorities dispatched an order to Johnston asking him to go to Beauregard's aid. Upon receiving the message early on July 18, Johnston called his brigade commanders together and informed them they would be moving toward Manassas Junction. Stuart was directed to take his cavalry north to demonstrate against Union forces north of Winchester in what would prove an eminently successful effort to dissuade them from disrupting or attempting to take advantage of Johnston's departure from the Valley.

Jackson's brigade, Johnston decided, would be the first to go to Beauregard's aid. Shortly after noon on July 18, Jackson and his men began marching out of Winchester toward the Blue Ridge. Upon reaching the Shenandoah River, which his command crossed at Berry's Ferry, Jackson ordered a member of his staff to ride on ahead to Piedmont Station on the Manassas Gap Railroad to arrange for the road's use. He then led his men over Ashby's Gap in the Blue Ridge before halting them around 2:00 A.M., at the small hamlet of Paris. As his men settled in for a well-deserved rest, Jackson walked through and around the camp before bedding down himself for the night—a legend would subsequently crop up out of this of that Jackson acted as a "lone sentry" while his men rested.

Jackson had his command on the road early enough on July 19 to cover the six miles from Paris to Piedmont Station by 8:00 A.M. They then boarded railroad cars for what would be an eight-hour trip covering the 34 miles from Piedmont Station to Manassas Junction. Upon reaching the Junction, Jackson immediately disembarked from the train and rode to Beauregard's headquarters to report his arrival and receive instructions. Beauregard directed him to post his command near Blackburn's Ford. One of the roads connecting Centreville, where McDowell was then concentrating his forces, with Manassas Junction crossed a stream called Bull Run at Blackburn's Ford, and on July 18 it had been the site of a sharp engagement between some of Beauregard's and McDowell's men. Jackson rode back to the junction and then led his men north through heavy rain showers to their assigned position in the Confederate line.

Though not completely accurate, Henry A. Ogden's painting dramatically captures the moment in the Battle of First Manassas (Bull Run) when Barnard Bee—the officer on horseback waving his hat—described Jackson as a "stone wall." (Library of Congress)

Jackson had his men up early on Sunday, July 21, but not as early as McDowell had his. At around 6:00 A.M., the sound of artillery and small arms fire could be heard upstream from Jackson's position. A little over three hours later Jackson received a message reporting that the Federals had crossed Bull Run a few miles above the Stone Bridge that carried the Warrenton Turnpike over the creek and marked the Confederate left—and his command was needed to help deal with the threat. Jackson responded with alacrity and quickly moved his command to the vicinity of the Stone Bridge but, after listening awhile to the sound of an intense fight to the west, ordered his command to move in that direction. At around noon, Jackson reached the eastern border of a large open plateau on which the home of Judith Henry sat.

Upon reaching Henry Hill, Jackson and his men were greeted with the sight of hundreds of bloodied and exhausted Confederate troops. Included among them was artillery Capt. John Imboden. From Imboden and other sources, Jackson learned that the brigades of Col. Nathan Evans from Beauregard's army and Brig. Gen. Bernard Bee's and Col. Francis Bartow's from Johnston's army had been overwhelmed after a tough fight on Matthews Hill with a massive Union force pushing south from a crossing of Bull Run located near Sudley Church. Imboden also reported that he had used his three guns to support their fight and cover their withdrawal but had been compelled to pull back. "I'll support your battery," Jackson replied, "Unlimber here." Imboden informed Jackson that he had nearly exhausted his ammunition in the course of the earlier engagement and intended to continue moving to the rear in search of ammunition to replenish his caissons, but Jackson persuaded him not to just yet.

Jackson then began methodically posting his five regiments in a tree-line in support of Imboden's position and, to bolster the position, brought up the four guns of the Rockbridge Artillery and two guns from a Richmond battery. Meanwhile, the forces that had been so roughly handled on Matthews Hill began to rally in the area behind the right of Jackson's line. One of their commanders, Bee, rode over to Jackson and excitedly reported, "General, they are driving us!" "Sir," Jackson sternly replied after quickly looking over the field, "we will give them the bayonet."

Fortunately for the Confederates, it was about this time that Mc-Dowell decided he needed to halt his infantry and consolidate his hold on Matthews Hill and the intersection of the Warrenton Turn-pike and Manassas-Sudley Road. Jackson took advantage of the pause in the Union infantry advance to establish and improve his position. Meanwhile, the Federals maintained a heavy artillery fire on Henry Hill, which resulted in Jackson receiving a minor wound in his hand. At around noon Beauregard and Johnston reached Henry Hill and approved Jackson's actions. They also decided to use his command as the foundation for a defensive line on the hill and began ordering up forces to assist Jackson.

The reinforcements Johnston and Beauregard began moving to Jackson's assistance would not arrive, however, until after McDowell resumed his advance shortly after 2:00 P.M. To open his attack on Jackson's line, which appeared to be all that stood in the way of a complete Union victory at Bull Run, McDowell ordered two artillery batteries forward to Henry Hill. Upon reaching the vicinity of the Henry House about 300 yards from Jackson's line, the Federal gunners unlimbered and began firing.

After a few minutes of exchanging fire with Jackson's gunners, one of the Union artillery commanders, Capt. Charles Griffin, decided to shift some of his guns to the right in an attempt to gain a position from which he could fire on the left flank of Jackson's line, which was held by Col. Arthur Cummings's 33rd Virginia. Meanwhile, McDowell moved up infantry to support them. Fortunately, recognizing the vulnerability of this end of his line, Jackson had persuaded Stuart to post some of his cavalry there to cover it. As the Federal infantry moved up, Stuart ordered a charge that threw them into confusion and left the Federal artillerists largely isolated.

Thus, the scene was set for the turning point of the First Battle of Manassas. Although Griffin was able to successfully post two guns on a small knoll just beyond Jackson's left flank, without adequate infantry support they were terribly vulnerable. Griffin had fired a few rounds from his new position when he caught sight of a body of armed men moving toward him. Correctly presuming they were Confederate, he ordered his gunners to fire on them. Before they could do so, however, one of McDowell's staff officers arrived on the scene and, convinced they were friendly due to the fact that some of the advancing forces were wearing blue uniforms (as was Jackson this day), countermanded the order. Consequently, the Confederates were able to approach within a hundred yards of Griffin's guns. They then halted, fired a terrific volley into the Federal position, and charged. Decimated physically, isolated from their comrades, and stunned by the sudden turn in events, Griffin's men were unable to put up much of a fight, and the Confederates were able to quickly overrun their position.

Shortly thereafter, though, McDowell finally managed to get infantry into the fight on this section of the field. After capturing Griffin's guns, organization in the units that had performed the feat quickly deteriorated as the men exulted in their conquest. Consequently, when a New York regiment showed upon the scene and fired into their position, they were unable to respond effectively and were compelled to fall back. The commander of the next regiment in Jackson's line, the 2nd Virginia, responded to this development by ordering the companies on his left to fall back to cover his flank. In the heat of battle, though, the order was misunderstood and the whole regiment began falling apart. Making matters worse, the commander of the 2nd Virginia was injured and lost control of his men.

One of Cummings's men raced over to Jackson and exclaimed, "General, the day is going against us." Jackson coolly responded, "If you think so, sir, you had better not say anything about it." He then rode over to the 4th and 27th Virginia and, as the New Yorkers advanced past Griffin's former position, steeled them for the coming clash. When the New Yorkers came into range, Jackson's men unleashed a storm of artillery and small arms fire that shattered their momentum and induced them to retreat.

Jackson immediately sensed that an opportunity had come to take the offensive and ordered the 4th and 27th Virginia forward. "We'll charge them now, and drive them back to Washington!" he shouted, "When you charge, yell like Furies!" Screaming what would become known as the "Rebel Yell," the two regiments, along with a North Carolina regiment that had just reached the field, pushed forward across the open plateau of Henry Hill and seized the Federal artillery line on Henry Hill, driving their crews back to the Sudley Road.

The day, however, was far from over. Shortly after the North Carolinians reached Griffin's position on the Confederate left, a regiment of Minnesota troops fired into their flank and forced them to fall back, enabling the Federals to remove Griffin's guns from the field. Meanwhile, McDowell ordered two Massachusetts regiments from Brig. Gen. William B. Franklin's brigade to recapture the battery of guns commanded by Capt. James B. Ricketts that were near the Henry House. Franklin's men were able to drive back Jackson's tired Virginians, but their success was short lived. At this point Beauregard personally ordered a charge by the 5th Virginia and some South Carolina troops that recaptured Ricketts's guns. Then, aided by elements from Bee's and Bartow's commands that had rallied and moved forward to rejoin the battle—although Bee and Bartow were both mortally wounded in the course of the fighting—Beauregard's and Jackson's men struggled to fight off a series of Federal attempts to recapture Ricketts's guns. Just as the Federals seemed to have gotten the upper hand, though, two regiments from Col. Philip St. George Cocke's Confederate brigade arrived on the field and effectively ended the fight for Henry Hill.

Meanwhile, both the Federal and Confederate commanders moved forces westward toward a section of high ground west of the Sudley Road known as Chinn Ridge. Just when it seemed the Federals had gotten the advantage on that part of the field, though, the last two brigades from Johnston's army arrived and routed the brigade of Federals that had seized Chinn Ridge. Realizing that nothing more could be achieved that day, McDowell ordered his men to retreat back to Centreville. The retreat, however, quickly degenerated into a rout as many of the inexperienced Federal troops panicked, and what had been a very closely fought battle was transformed into a sweeping, decisive victory for the Confederacy.

With the possible exception of Beauregard, no one stood higher than Jackson in post-battle accounts, and deservedly so. His generalship and management of his command on Henry Hill both defensively and offensively had been critical in transforming what at the beginning of the day seemed destined to be a crushing—and perhaps war-ending—defeat for the Confederacy into a grand victory. Jackson's place, and that of his brigade, in the hearts and minds of the Confederate faithful received a decided boost from reports after the battle that at its height, Bee had rallied his men by pointing to Jackson's line on Henry Hill and shouting, "Look men, there is Jackson standing like a stone wall!" Henceforth, he would be known as Stonewall Jackson. His brigade, which had lost nearly 500 men in the battle—roughly 16 percent of its effective force—would be known from that point forward as the Stonewall Brigade.

Chapter 5

VALLEY COMMANDER

RETURN TO THE VALLEY

As the sounds of battle faded on July 21, 1861, Jackson made his way to a field hospital at the insistence of General Johnston to get his wound treated. As he did so, a sense that an opportunity existed to make the victory even more decisive through aggressive action increasingly dominated his thinking. Lamentably for the Confederacy, the disorganized state of its army after the battle and the speed with which the Federals got back to Washington proved to be insurmountable obstacles to such a course of action.

Thus, the days after the battle were spent settling back into the routine of camp, the challenge of which was exacerbated by heavy rains. These made the poorly sited camp the Stonewall Brigade was assigned near Bull Run a morass and led Jackson, whose wound became infected, to request permission to relocate his camp. This was granted, and during the first week of August the brigade moved to a new camp near Centreville. There, Jackson endeavored to reinstitute the strict discipline that had become his trademark.

Early September brought a visit from Jackson's wife to the camp. She later recalled seeing that "General Jackson was justly proud of his brigade, and their affection for him was beautiful to behold. They all felt so inspirited by the great victory they had just gained, and their general's part in it was rehearsed with pride by everyone who called upon his wife." This was followed shortly thereafter by relocation of the brigade's camp further east to an encampment just outside Fairfax Court House.

While Jackson and his brigade were encamped there, Confederate president Jefferson Davis arrived to discuss strategy with Johnston and Beauregard. During a meeting with Davis, Jackson pressed upon the president the need for aggressive operations in the northwestern section of Virginia to drive out Federal troops in the region, but he was disappointed by the negative response his proposal received. Instead of the vigorous offensive operations Jackson was eager to undertake (at one point during this time he argued for crossing the Potomac with visions of destroying Federal armies, industrial establishments, cities, and resource areas as far north as the "neck of country between Pittsburgh and Lake Erie" swirling in his head) the next major development operationally in Virginia proved to be a retrograde movement of Confederate forces back to Centreville in response to some tentative Federal offensives just outside Washington.

More positively, in October Jackson learned that he had been promoted to major general and given command of a division in Johnston's army. Shortly thereafter, the Confederate War Department announced a reorganization of its forces in northern Virginia. The newly organized Department of Northern Virginia, under Johnston's command, would consist of three districts. Jackson was the natural choice to command the new Valley district in the minds of the residents of the area who petitioned for his appointment, which was made during the second half of October. This necessitated separation from the Stonewall Brigade, which was retained in northeastern Virginia as part of Beauregard's Potomac district. "Officers and men of the First Brigade!" an evidently—and uncharacteristically—emotional Jackson exclaimed to the men of his former brigade just before departing for Winchester on November 4, "You were the First Brigade in the Army of the Shenandoah, the First Brigade in the Army of the Potomac . . . and are the First Brigade in the hearts of your generals. I hope that you will be the First Brigade in this, our second struggle for independence, and in the future, on the fields on which the Stonewall Brigade are engaged, I expect to hear of crowning deeds of valor and of victories gloriously achieved! May God bless you all! Farewell!"

Jackson and his staff arrived in Winchester early on November 5 and immediately went to work. When he arrived the Federals had a force of about 4,000 at Romney, with thousands more dispersed elsewhere in the section of the Shenandoah Valley north of Winchester. To defend the Valley, Jackson had less than 2,000 men in his command, few of whom were well armed or trained. A call for more militia to assemble at Winchester immediately upon his arrival added another thousand, but this was still far too few for Jackson to hope to put up much of a defense against the Federals. Things brightened considerably, though, when the War Department acquiesced to Jackson's request for the Stonewall Brigade to be transferred to his command. This development was warmly welcomed by both Jackson and his men, although it did not take long for the former's trademark insistence on strict discipline to grate on some of the men and lead to several arrests. Among the officers giving Jackson trouble was Col. James Allen, his successor as the brigade's commander, which led to Richmond assigning command of the unit to Brig. Gen. Richard B. Garnett in early December.

THE ROMNEY EXPEDITION

Despite his problems, Jackson badly wished to take the offensive against the Federals. On November 20 he sent a letter to Richmond requesting that the three-brigade force commanded by Brig. Gen. William W. Loring, then posted in the mountainous region of western Virginia to defend the approaches to Staunton, be ordered to Winchester. Once reinforced, Jackson proposed to strike at a Federal force then occupying Romney. After soliciting the opinions of Johnston and Lee on the proposal, Secretary of War Judah Benjamin wrote to Loring to suggest he move his force to Winchester. Loring agreed to do so, but expressed reservations about Jackson's plan in light of how late in the season it was. His concerns proved well-founded, for the weeks that followed would offer a vivid demonstration of just how difficult winter campaigning in the mountains of northwestern Virginia could be.

Upon learning that Richmond had ordered Loring to join him, Jackson immediately began planning in earnest for a move against Romney. He badgered officials in the War Department and Virginia state government to prod Loring to move faster to join him. Although Loring had still not arrived, Jackson decided on December 7 to order a small force to move north of Martinsburg to destroy Dam No. 5 on the Chesapeake and Ohio Canal. The raid failed to achieve its objectives and Jackson subsequently moved up to Martinsburg and set up his headquarters there. On December 17 he ordered another raid against Dam No. 5, this time by a larger force under his personal command. This time he was more successful, although the damage to the dam was rather quickly repaired.

After returning to Winchester, Jackson was able to enjoy the company of his wife while he waited for Loring's force. Finally, on December 24, Loring personally reached Winchester, with the last of his command arriving three days later. Loring's three brigades brought the size of Jackson's force to four brigades of about 11,000 men in all. Early on January 1, which proved to be an unusually warm New Year's Day in that part of Virginia, Jackson's long-awaited offensive against Romney began.

When the march began, spirits were high among Jackson's men. But then, as the terrain became increasingly rugged, a brutally cold wind began sweeping into the region. As if this were not bad enough, Jackson's chief logistician had fallen ill before the march began and been forced to remain behind in Winchester. Without him, the wagons accompanying Jackson's column became badly disorganized, depriving the men of food, blankets, and other needed equipment on the brutally cold night of January 1–2. The next day a swirling snow began to fall on Jackson's hungry men as they resumed their march. Making matters worse, Jackson on the advice of his doctor decided to consume some brandy, which impaired his ability to appreciate just how cold it was. Thus, he continued to drive his men forward without food or shelter.

Fortunately that evening the wagon train caught up with Jackson's men at their bivouac at Unger's Store. Then, however, Jackson learned to his intense dismay that Loring had decided to halt his command's march that day short of Unger's Store, which Jackson had designated for its stopping point that day. Loring then rode forward to headquarters and was subjected to a tongue lashing from Jackson, who wanted his forces up that evening so they would be in position to attack a Union garrison at Bath the next day. A furious Loring returned to his men and, as he moved to comply with Jackson's wishes, shouted out in front of the men that "this is the damndest outrage ever perpetrated in the annals of history, keeping my men out here in the cold without food!"

The following morning Garnett felt Jackson's wrath. Determined to begin the march on Bath immediately, Jackson refused to let the men of the Stonewall Brigade, who had not eaten in over a day, fully consume the rations they were finally able to draw from the supply wagons. Garnett defied Jackson's wishes and let the men cook their rations. When he found out about Garnett's actions, Jackson immediately made his way over to his headquarters. When Garnett attempted to explain the very good reasons behind his decision to a manifestly irate Jackson, Stonewall exclaimed, "There is no time for that!" Garnett then protested that it would be impossible for the men to march if they did not get fed properly. Jackson coldly rebuked him by replying, "I never found anything impossible with this brigade."

Garnett's men shortly thereafter joined the rest of Jackson's command as it pushed forward in two wings toward Bath. Jackson's hope of taking the garrison by surprise was foiled, though, when the pickets made contact and began firing. Loring then countermanded an order from Jackson to his lead brigade calling for an immediate attack, which provoked another bitter argument between the two men. That night a heavy snow fell on Jackson's exposed men, who not surprisingly performed abysmally in the final advance on Bath on January 4. To Jackson's immense frustration, this allowed the bulk of its garrison to escape before the Confederates were able to claim possession of the town. Making matters worse for the Confederates, that night the temperature dropped even further and Jackson's command were forced to endure a horrible night miserably huddled around fires.

The following day, some of the Confederates managed to burn a bridge and tear up some railroad track, while others made an effort on

Jackson's orders to attack the Federal garrison at Hancock, Maryland. For two days, Jackson's men would fire on the town in an attempt to compel its surrender, but the high Potomac River and the arrival of Federal reinforcements frustrated the attempt. Finally, on the morning of January 7 Jackson ordered his men to return to Unger's Store, where he planned to regroup before pushing on to Romney. A snowstorm fell throughout the day that brutally punished the men and animals in Jackson's force as they straggled back to Unger's Store. Jackson and his men then spent four miserably cold and hungry days there, during which Jackson wrote to Richmond expressing his discontent with Garnett and belief that he needed to be relieved from command. Richmond ignored the suggestion.

On January 12, as Jackson completed his preparations for an advance on Romney, a report from cavalry commander Col. Turner Ashby arrived stating that the Federals had already evacuated the town. The following day, Jackson put his command on the march through mud produced by a brief thaw that was followed the next evening by snow. Nonetheless, on January 14 Jackson's command reached Romney, with the Stonewall Brigade in the vanguard, and claimed possession of the town and the tens of thousands of dollars worth of stores the Federals had left behind when they evacuated. Jackson immediately hatched a plan for continuing his offensive, but his command was too physically and morally exhausted to do so. Thus, he ordered the Stonewall Brigade back to Winchester to take up winter quarters and instructed Loring's men to do the same at Romney. Jackson accompanied the former and by the end of January was back at Winchester with his wife.

Not surprisingly, the Romney expedition and Jackson's handling of his command quickly became a matter of controversy in Richmond. Loring and his officers were understandably—and justifiably—furious at the callous disregard for the health of the men with which Jackson, who spent most nights during the operation indoors while his men suffered in the cold, wind, and snow, had conducted the campaign. They were further dismayed by Jackson's decision to leave their command at Romney while he and the Stonewall Brigade had been allowed to return to Winchester. One of Loring's brigadiers traveled to Richmond and gained audiences with several high government officials, including President Jefferson Davis and Vice-President Alexander Stephens, during which he bitterly denounced Jackson. In late January, General Johnston received directions from Richmond to investigate matters in the Valley District. A few days later, the War Department sent a message to Jackson directing him to order Loring's men back to Winchester.

Jackson did not appreciate Richmond interfering in matters related to his command that he believed were his exclusive purview. He grudgingly complied with the order but also informed Richmond that, "With such interference in my command I cannot expect to be of much service in the field; and accordingly respectfully request to be ordered to report for duty to the Superintendent of the Virginia Military Institute. . . . Should this application not be granted, I respectfully request that the President will accept my resignation from the Army." Jackson then wrote a letter to Virginia governor John Letcher asking him to use his authority to arrange his return to VMI and complaining about Richmond's order, which he proclaimed "an attempt to control military operations in detail from the Secretary's [of War] desk at a distance. . . . I take for granted that he has done what he believed to be best but I regard such a policy as ruinous."

When Johnston learned what Jackson was doing, he made a vigorous effort to get Jackson to reconsider his actions. "I don't know how the loss of this officer," he advised the War Department, "can be supplied." Meanwhile, Congressman Alexander Boteler personally called on Secretary of War Benjamin and President Davis to press Jackson's case. He asked them not to act on Jackson's request and recruited Governor Letcher to assist in the effort. Boteler then traveled to Winchester to personally appeal to Jackson not to resign. In the course of their conversation Jackson strongly reiterated his determination to serve the Confederacy and wish not to leave his command in what he believed to be a critical theater of the war. "If this Valley is lost," he exclaimed, "Virginia is lost."

Two days after this conversation, Jackson notified Letcher that he wished to withdraw his resignation. The whole episode might have ended peacefully there, but the ink on Jackson's letter to Letcher had barely dried when he decided to go after Loring by ordering a court martial to try the officer on seven charges. To Jackson's dismay, though, there would be no trial. Davis and Benjamin wisely decided to defuse the whole situation by reorganizing Jackson's forces and reassigning Loring and much of his command elsewhere.

While disappointed at this development, Jackson nonetheless had a major cause for cheer in February 1862. In addition to maintaining a warm and comfortable residence, that month Mary Anna Jackson became pregnant. Meanwhile, Jackson continued to manage his command while also finding time to engage socially with some of the leading members of Winchester society.

One night while relaxing with a local minister he had befriended, Jackson held forth on the conduct of war. "War means fighting," he declared, "The business of a soldier is to fight. Armies are not called out to dig trenches, to throw up breastworks, and live in camps, but to find the enemy, and strike him; to invade his country, and do him all the possible damage in the shortest possible time." When his friend expressed concern at the violence and destruction inherent in such an approach to war, Jackson replied that in fact his approach would be less damaging in the long run. "Such a war," he explained, "would of necessity be of brief countenance, and so would be an economy of prosperity and life in the end." "To move swiftly, strike vigorously, and secure all the fruits of victory," he added, "is the secret of successful war."

In a conversation with a subordinate during the first year of the war, Jackson further elaborated on his military philosophy. There were two things, he declared, that no military commander should ever lose sight of. The first was to, "Always mystify, mislead, and surprise the enemy, if possible; when you strike and overcome him, never let up in the pursuit so long as your men have strength to follow." The second was to "never fight against heavy odds, if by any possible maneuvering you can hurl your own force on only a part, and that the weakest part, of your enemy and crush it. Such tactics will win every time." The months that followed would demonstrate just how much "Stonewall" Jackson believed in such an approach to war.

Chapter 6

WE SHALL GET
THEM ON THE RUN

KERNSTOWN

The 1862 campaign season in the Shenandoah Valley began in earnest in early March. The commander of the main Union army in Virginia, Maj. Gen. George B. McClellan, had won very grudging approval from President Abraham Lincoln for an operation that would take his massive Army of the Potomac to the Lower Chesapeake Bay. The army would then advance on Richmond from the east, moving up the rivers that flowed into the bay. Lincoln's reluctance to let McClellan carry out his well-conceived plan was rooted in anxiety over the security of Washington when the Army of the Potomac was away. Of particular concern to Lincoln was that the lower Shenandoah Valley be secured, as it offered a convenient invasion route into Maryland and Pennsylvania.

To ensure this was done, in early March a considerable Federal force commanded by Maj. Gen. Nathaniel P. Banks crossed the Potomac River to secure Harpers Ferry and then pushed south up the Shenandoah Valley. By March 7, Banks's command had advanced to a point about five miles north of Winchester. There it made contact with Jackson's cavalry force, commanded by Col. Turner Ashby, and pushed it back to a point approximately two miles north of the town. There Banks halted his command and began probing toward Winchester with a sensibly fair degree of caution.

The same day Banks made contact with Ashby's cavalry, Johnston began moving the Confederate forces at Manassas and Centreville south to a more defensible position behind the Rappahannock River. Banks's advance had the opposite effect on Jackson. He immediately began thinking offensively, even though his command of less than 4,000 soldiers was considerably outnumbered by Banks's. Jackson hatched a plan for a surprise attack on March 11, but when misdirected wagons and the opposition of his subordinates prevented its execution, he concluded he had no choice but to evacuate Winchester and withdraw south up the Shenandoah Valley. By March 20 Jackson's command had fallen back about 40 miles before halting to take up a position a few miles northeast of Mount Jackson.

As Jackson was doing this, McClellan had begun moving his army to the Lower Chesapeake. As part of McClellan's plan for securing Washington, and with Jackson's force presumed to be neutralized, Banks received orders to begin shifting part of his command east of the Blue Ridge to Manassas Junction. Banks then ordered the division commanded by Brig. Gen. James Shields that had pushed south to Strasburg to begin pulling back to Winchester so that the move east could begin.

On March 21, Jackson learned from Ashby that Shields was moving down the Shenandoah Valley toward Winchester, and Banks had begun moving a large body of wagons east toward the Blue Ridge. Seeing a long-hoped-for opportunity to strike the Federals a successful blow, and having received a March 19 letter from Johnston stating, "Would not your presence with your troops nearer Winchester prevent the enemy from diminishing his force there? . . . . Do try to prevent it by getting and keeping as near as prudence will permit," Jackson immediately issued orders to his men to move north. On March 22, Jackson pushed his command over 20 miles to the vicinity of Strasburg, while Ashby's cavalry fought a vigorous skirmish with part of Shields's command, in which Shields suffered a bad injury to his arm. After the fight ended, Ashby sent Jackson reports of what had happened that badly underestimated the strength of Shields's command.

His eagerness to strike at the Federals further stoked, Jackson put his command on the march for Winchester early on March 23. Ashby's cavalry and Garnett's Stonewall Brigade soon reached the outskirts of Kernstown, a small hamlet about four miles south of Winchester on the Valley Turnpike. Initially disinclined to further pursue his efforts that day on account of the fact that it was a Sunday, Jackson quickly set aside his reservations and decided to attack. "[T]hough very distasteful to my feelings," he later explained to his wife, "I felt it my duty to do it, in consideration of the ruinous effects that might result from postponing the battle."

Federal artillery posted on a piece of high ground west of the turnpike known as Pritchard's Hill had a clear view of Jackson's command and, the Confederate commander understood, would pose a serious menace to his force as if it continued moving north along the Valley Pike. Moreover, possession of Pritchard's Hill would give Jackson's command access to ground from which it might turn the right flank of any Federal forces in the area. Assured by Ashby that the Federals could not have more than a brigade in the vicinity of Winchester, a force large enough to make for a nice little victory if they could be whipped but not large enough to be really dangerous, Jackson decided to attack.

At around 2:00 P.M., Jackson had his command of about 3,000 infantry arranged to his satisfaction and ordered them begin the attack. While Ashby's cavalry demonstrated against Federal forces along the Valley Turnpike, Jackson directed the two regiments of Col. Samuel Fulkerson's brigade to move about a half mile west of the turnpike and then advance north to turn the Union position on Pritchard's Hill, with the Stonewall Brigade in support.

The situation, however, was not quite what Jackson thought it was. The Federals, it turned out, were much stronger than Ashby had reported. Making matters worse, when Fulkerson led his command to a point at the base of Pritchard's Hill, Federal artillery was able to pound his ranks with a ferocious fire. Jackson ordered 13 cannon to move west to Sandy Ridge with two regiments of infantry in support, hoping they could suppress the Union artillery. Col. Nathan Kimball, the Union commander on the field, responded by dispatching a brigade commanded by Col. Erastus B. Tyler to Sandy Ridge. The arrival of Tyler's brigade and the piecemeal manner with which Jackson shifted forces over to Sandy Ridge fatally compromised whatever hopes Jackson might have had that he could turn the Federal right, although Tyler's efforts to accomplish more by launching attacks of his own were also unsuccessful. Meanwhile, the men of Garnett's command found themselves in a tough fight in which the weight of superior Federal numbers quickly began to take a toll on the Stonewall Brigade.

Recognizing that his command was in serious trouble, Jackson ordered reinforcements to assist Garnett and Fulkerson and rode among their men to urge them on, directing one soldier who had run low on ammunition to "go back and give them the bayonet." Before Jackson could get reinforcements to Garnett, though, his command was running low on ammunition and facing the prospect of being overwhelmed. Thus, at around 6:00 P.M., Garnett on his own initiative ordered his men to disengage and pull back. Fulkerson had no choice but to fall back also.

As the triumphant Federals surged forward to complete their victory, the Confederate retreat quickly disintegrated into a rout. Jackson was furious and directed his anger at Garnett. As he rode forward to find Garnett vainly trying to rally his old brigade, Jackson bluntly interrogated him. "Why have you not rallied your men?" he asked Garnett. Unsatisfied with Garnett's explanation, Jackson tried to personally rally the men, but it was no use. Still, Jackson made a point of remaining on the field until after night fell, along with two regiments that had come up and managed to hold a final line, thanks in part to the fading daylight. He then followed his broken command as it staggered into Bartonsville, having lost 139 killed and mortally wounded, 312 wounded, and 286 captured or missing at Kernstown—in all nearly a quarter of his engaged force.

That evening a young artillerist provided Jackson with a colloquial but accurate assessment of the day's events. "General," he declared, "it looks like you cut off more tobacco today than you could chew." A few days later, one of Fulkerson's men was far less charitable. "General Jackson," he complained to his family, "was completely taken in. The wonder is why the Yankees didn't capture our whole army."

While Shields, Kimball, and their men celebrated their victory on March 24 and the Confederates continued their retreat south up the Shenandoah Valley toward Rude's Hill, an angry and embarrassed

Jackson turned his wrath on Garnett. While conceding his force had fought at a disadvantage, Jackson complained in his report on the battle that if Garnett had not ordered his command to pull back when he did, "the enemy's advance would at least have been retarded, and the remaining part of my Infantry reserve have had a better opportunity for coming up." Five days after Kernstown, Jackson wrote to his superiors to ask them to send a new brigadier to the Valley. He then formally relieved Garnett of command and placed him under arrest, charging him with mismanagement in how he positioned his command at Kernstown, failing to stay with and properly manage his command during the battle, and ordering a retreat without proper authorization. Garnett was, he proclaimed, "so incompetent a Brigade commander . . . that, instead of building up a Brigade, a good one, if turned over to him, would actually deteriorate."

The men of the Stonewall Brigade disagreed. They vehemently objected to the arrest of Garnett, who indignantly—and with full confidence that he would be vindicated—demanded that the trial Jackson called for be convened immediately. Their anger was further stoked when Richmond chose Brig. Gen. Charles Sidney Winder, a Marylander and an outsider, to replace Garnett, rather than promoting someone from within the brigade, and expressed their dismay by openly hissing when Winder arrived to assume command. As they labored to recover from Kernstown, Jackson and Winder clearly had much work to do.

Yet, however depressing the result of the engagement at Kernstown may have seemed in the Confederate camps in late March, the battle actually proved to be of great positive significance for the Confederacy— and must be deemed one of the great turning points of the Civil War. Even though his command suffered a decisive tactical defeat, the fact that Jackson had the audacity to attack Shields's force so spooked the Lincoln administration that it decided to withhold troops originally designated for service in the grand campaign against Richmond that had commenced the week before Kernstown.

To guard Washington and allow Banks's command to remain in the Valley to watch Jackson, Lincoln decided to withhold from Mc-Clellan the largest corps in his army and keep it in northern Virginia. This forced McClellan to shelve a plan for a quick operation against a Confederate defensive position at Yorktown in favor of a month-long siege operation that would give the Confederates time to plot even more mischief in the Shenandoah Valley.

McDOWELL

Nonetheless, not being privy to just how badly the Lincoln administration had been scared, early April 1862 was a gloomy time for Jackson. Not only did he have to rehabilitate his command after it was so badly roughed up at Kernstown, but he learned that Johnston had been compelled to abandon the position he had taken up along the Rapidan and Rappahannock rivers and move to the York-James Peninsula to deal with McClellan's operations there. There was, however, a silver lining in this. Jackson and the commander of the lone division Johnston had left behind along the Rapidan-Rappahannock, Brig. Gen. Richard S. Ewell, were told that Jackson was authorized to order Ewell's command to the Shenandoah Valley if he deemed it necessary. While he also received orders to prepare to pull back farther up the Valley to place himself in a better position to link up with Ewell, the prospect of being reinforced aroused hopes on Jackson's part that he might soon have the means to once again take the offensive.

Jackson immediately made contact with Ewell and began moving his command south up the Valley toward Harrisonburg to facilitate a rendezvous with Ewell's command. After reaching Harrisonburg, Jackson and his men then moved east around the southern end of Massanutten, the 50-mile long mountain range that separates the Shenandoah Valley and Luray Valley. He then halted his command at Conrad's Store, which placed it east of Massanutten Mountain, near the southern end of the Luray Valley, and close to Swift Run Gap in the Blue Ridge. Upon reaching Conrad's Store on April 19, Jackson's men were in a convenient location to link up with Ewell, who had received orders two days earlier to march his division toward the Blue Ridge.

Meanwhile, Banks's forces pushed south up the Valley west of Massanutten Mountain toward Harrisonburg. Believing Jackson's fleeing command was no longer a serious threat, Banks looked forward to eventually reaching Staunton. This would facilitate cooperation with Federal forces commanded by Maj. Gen. John C. Fremont, which were then in the mountains of western Virginia and had orders to move east to the Shenandoah Valley.

It was the approach of advanced elements of Fremont's command toward the Shenandoah Valley along the Staunton-Parkersburg Turnpike that spurred Jackson to resume active operations. He made this decision confident that he was acting in accordance with the wishes of General Robert E. Lee, who had just assumed the post of chief military advisor to President Jefferson Davis. On April 21 Lee advised Jackson that he believed the greatest danger to the Confederate effort in Virginia was the prospect that Federal forces commanded by Maj. Gen. Irvin McDowell that had been held back from McClellan's command in the aftermath of Kernstown would march south overland from Fredericksburg to link up with McClellan around Richmond.

To thwart this, Lee suggested offensive action. Two days later, Jackson replied to Lee's message and announced he would attempt to strike Banks's force the first chance he could. Lee wrote back to Jackson that all Confederate forces available for use in the Valley—then divided among Jackson's force of about 8,400 at Conrad's Store, Ewell's division of 8,000 on the other side of Swift Run Gap, and a force of around 3,000 commanded by Brig. Gen. Edward Johnson defending the western approach to Staunton along the Staunton-Parkersburg Pike—should be concentrated. This would ensure a strong blow could be delivered in line with Lee's admonition that "The blow wherever struck, must, to be successful, be sudden and heavy."

Banks's force of about 19,000 men began arriving at Harrisonburg on April 24; however, the leisurely character of its march up the Valley and inactivity after reaching Harrisonburg suggested that it had little interest in aggressive operations at that point. The same was not the case with Fremont's force, whose advanced element of 6,000 men, led by Brig. Gen. Robert H. Milroy, was then menacing Johnson's position west of Staunton. Upon sizing up the situation, Jackson quickly decided to order Ewell's command to Conrad's Store. This would allow Jackson to take his men west to link up with Johnson and attempt to strike a blow at Milroy. On April 28, Ewell personally reached Conrad's Store and received his directions from Jackson. As the men of Ewell's division made their way over the Blue Ridge, early on the morning of April 30 Jackson put his men on the march.

Jackson's men first moved east over the Blue Ridge, with their commander hoping to persuade Banks that he was going to reinforce Richmond and there was little to worry about in the Valley. In fact, Jackson was heading to Meachum's River Station, on the railroad connecting Richmond and Staunton. After a hard march occasionally accompanied by heavy rains, on May 4 Jackson placed his sick and injured soldiers on cars that would take them west to Staunton and ordered the rest of his command to march along the road. This was greatly to the delight of the men, who, not being privy to the plans of their intensely secretive commander, had initially feared that they were in fact abandoning the Valley. "That [the train] was to be taken to Richmond when the troops were all embarked no one doubted," one officer later recalled, "With sad and gloomy hearts, they boarded the trains at Meachum's Station. When all were on, lo! they took a westward course."

That same day, Jackson received word from Johnson that Milroy's force was approaching Staunton quicker than had earlier been reported. More positively, he learned that Banks was moving north back down the Valley to New Market in order to shorten his lines of communication and supplies. On May 5, Jackson and his command reached Staunton and received an exuberant welcome from its residents. Two days later, after taking a day to rest and prepare for what promised to be a tough march through mountainous terrain that one officer later proclaimed "the meanest country I ever saw," Jackson and his command departed Staunton. Before doing so, though, the general finally got a chance to, a staff officer reported in his diary, lay "aside the blue (U.S.) Major's uniform which he had worn at the V.M.I. and continued to wear up to this time, and put on a full new suit of Confederate grey."

Early on May 8, Jackson, accompanied by cartographer Jedediah Hotchkiss, reached a point on the Staunton Pike about three miles from the town of McDowell. Hotchkiss then guided Jackson over to a high point south of the pike known as Sitlington's Hill, which overlooked McDowell. There he encountered General Johnson, whose skirmishers already had made contact with Milroy's force. Although the Confederates enjoyed a commanding defensive position, Jackson had little interest in merely fighting a defensive battle. After looking over the situation and talking with Johnson, Jackson asked Hotchkiss to see if he could find some way to reach and attack the rear of Milroy's forces.

Before Hotchkiss could do so, though, Milroy ordered a direct assault on Sitlington's Hill. Johnson quickly finished posting his command on the hill and immediately began putting up a fierce resistance against the gallant, but outnumbered Federal attackers. When the sound of the fighting reached Jackson, who had ridden back to the rear to take supper with his staff, he immediately ordered two brigades to the front to assist Johnson. Shortly thereafter, a wagon carrying a wounded Johnson reached Jackson. After a brief conversation with Johnson, Jackson told Hotchkiss to ride to the front. "Go up to Gen. [William B.] Taliaferro," Jackson directed, "and give him my compliments and tell him I am coming in person with the Stonewall Brigade and he must hold his position until I come."

By the time Jackson reached the field, though, night had fallen, and the Federals, having failed in their attempt to seize Sitlington's Hill, had pulled back to McDowell. Early on May 9, Jackson learned Milroy had evacuated McDowell and was moving west to rejoin the rest of Fremont's force at Franklin. Upon occupying McDowell and setting up his headquarters, Jackson had a message sent to Richmond announcing, "God blessed our arms with victory at McDowell." Jackson hoped to accomplish more, but, exhausted from their exertions at McDowell, his men were in no condition to launch much of a pursuit the day after the battle, although by May 12 Jackson had pushed his forces to the outskirts of Franklin. There he found Fremont's command too strongly posted to hope to accomplish anything against it. The following day, satisfied that he had neutralized Fremont's force, and anxious to get back to Banks's force in the Valley, Jackson ordered his men to begin moving back to Staunton.

This came not a moment too soon. Even though Banks had pulled back to New Market, Ewell had grown increasingly and understandably anxious due to the ever secretive Jackson's failure to keep him fully informed of his plans. While the McDowell operation was taking place, Ewell exploded during a meeting with Col. James A. Walker, asking Walker if it "ever occur[ed] to you that General Jackson is crazy?" Walker replied that when he had been a student at VMI, "We used to called him Tom Fool Jackson . . . but I don't suppose he is really crazy."

Ewell disagreed. "I tell you, sir, he is as crazy as a March hare! He has gone away, I don't know where, and left me here with some instructions to stay until he returns, but Banks's whole army is advancing on me and I haven't the most remote idea where to communicate with General Jackson! I tell you, sir, he is crazy and I will just march my division away from here! I do not mean to have it cut to pieces at the behest of a crazy man!"

Shortly thereafter, Ewell learned that not only was Banks not advancing, but that he had ordered one of his divisions, Shields's, the one that had so roughly handled Jackson's command at Kernstown, east to Fredericksburg. If allowed to do this unhindered, this promised great mischief for the Confederate war effort in Virginia, for if Shields were able to reach Fredericksburg and reinforce the Federal force there that was preparing to march south to join McClellan outside Richmond, the Confederate capital was all but certain to fall.

This news also served to further exacerbate Ewell's frustration with Jackson. Believing he had an opportunity that was being squandered while Jackson was off chasing Federal wagons, Ewell exclaimed to a subordinate that, "We are left out here in the cold! Why, I could crush Shields before night if I could move from here! This man Jackson is certainly a crazy fool, an idiot!"

CRUSHING BANKS

At that moment, though, Jackson was already moving east from Mc-Dowell. It was a hard march, through what seemed to be unceasing rain, and while it was underway Jackson sent a message to Ewell on May 13 advising him to get ready for active operations. "If Banks goes down the [V]alley," Jackson wrote, "I wish you to follow him; so that he may feel that if he leaves the Valley, that not only will we occupy it, but that he will also be liable to be attacked so soon as he shall have sufficiently weakened his forces." On May 15, Lee's aide in Richmond wrote to Ewell to inform him "that you need not feel any further solicitude on account of General Jackson, [General Lee] having been informed by telegram that he is returning to Staunton, and is probably there by this time. . . . The general thinks that if upon the junction of yours and General Jackson's forces a blow could be struck at Banks it would make a happy diversion in our favor."

Lee wrote to Jackson directly the next day to advise him of reports that a significant portion of Banks's command was moving east. This suggested to Lee that "Banks may intend to move his army to the Manassas Junction and march thence to Fredericksburg, or he may design going to Alexandria and proceeding thence by water either to Fredericksburg or, as I think more probable, to the Peninsula to re-enforce McClellan." Lee then declared, "Whatever may be Banks's intention it is very desirable to prevent him from going either to Fredericksburg or to the Peninsula. A successful blow struck at him would delay, if it does not prevent, his moving to either place." "Whatever movements you make against Banks," Lee advised, "do it speedily, and if successful, drive him towards the Potomac, and create the impression as far as practicable that you design threatening that line."

Jackson eagerly seized on the authorization for offensive operations contained in Lee's letter. On May 17, he ordered Ewell to begin moving north down the Luray Valley so he could reach a position from which he could menace any forces Banks was moving east toward the Blue Ridge. That same day, though, Ewell received a message from Joseph E. Johnston, written on May 13, that directed him to instead prepare to move east to join the forces defending Richmond. The message was also sent to Jackson, who immediately replied that he was at that moment "moving down the Valley for the purpose of striking Banks; but the withdrawal of Genl. Ewell's command will prevent my purpose being executed. . . . If I do not hear from you soon I will continue my march."

The next day, Ewell went to Jackson's headquarters and proposed continuing their operations until they received a response to Jackson's message of the day before. They agreed that the fact that Lee's message urging offensive operations against Banks had been drafted later than Johnston's meant that it superseded the directive to move to Richmond. Thus, the following morning, the advance against Banks continued in earnest. Two of Ewell's brigades moved north down the Luray Valley east of Massanutten Mountain, while Ewell's third brigade moved north from Harrisonburg west of the mountain with the rest of Jackson's command.

After making good progress in his march down the Shenandoah Valley on May 19, Jackson was understandably taken aback the following morning when he received a message from Johnston directing him to send Ewell to Richmond. Jackson immediately wrote to Lee to protest the order and instructed Ewell not to execute Johnston's order until they had gotten Lee's response. Upon receiving Jackson's message, Lee went to President Davis and successfully pressed to keep Ewell in the Valley. By nightfall, messages from Lee and Johnston were on their way to Jackson acceding to his wishes.

On May 21, Jackson's force turned east and crossed Massanutten Mountain at New Market Gap. Upon reaching the Luray Valley, Jackson linked up his command with Ewell's and informed his subordinates that he planned to move their entire force north to Front Royal. Reaching Front Royal would enable them to turn Banks's fortified position, located 12 miles to the west at Strasburg. It would also block Federal efforts to continue shifting units over the Blue Ridge to Fredericksburg, where the Federal high command was then planning and organizing a march of the forces there south to join McClellan outside Richmond. Seizing Front Royal would also place Jackson's forces in a position from which they would pose such a menace to Banks's line of communication back to the Potomac River that the Federal commander would have no choice but to retreat or fight at a severe disadvantage.

If Jackson was hoping for an opportunity to win a quick, easy, confidence-boosting victory, he could hardly have asked for a better situation than the one he found at Front Royal on May 23. The only Federal force there was a band of about a thousand troops commanded by Col. John Kenly. Upon reaching Spangler's Crossroads a few miles from the town, Jackson split his force of about 14,000, sending a portion of his cavalry west, while Ewell's command moved to the north and east and the rest of Jackson's command advanced on Front Royal from the south.

As they advanced, the vanguard of Jackson's command, the brigade commanded by Brig. Gen. Richard Taylor, easily swept aside the skirmishers Kenly had thrown out. As Jackson's men entered Front Royal, Kenly responded by pulling back to a piece of high ground known as Richardson's Hill, where he supported his small infantry force with two pieces of artillery. As they cleared the town, Jackson's infantry deployed into line while his artillery commander Col. Stapleton Crutch-field searched for artillery with enough range to counter the Federal guns. By the time Crutchfield managed to do so, however, Jackson's infantry had overwhelmed Kenly's position. Meanwhile, Ashby's cavalry cut the telegraph line connecting Kenly with Banks at Strasburg, then pushed east to menace Kenly's line of retreat. Kenly had no choice but to retreat across the North and South Forks of the Shenandoah River toward Winchester and attempt to burn the bridges behind him.

Jackson's men were able to save the bridges, though, and, with their commander personally urging them on, continued to pursue Kenly with a force of cavalry commanded by Lt. Col. Thomas Flournoy in the lead. The Federals had not gotten three miles from the crossing of the North Fork of the Shenandoah when the pressure of Flournoy's pursuit became so great that Kenly decided he had to make another stand near the village of Cedarville. Kenly's men were only able to get off a single shot, though, before their position astride the road linking Winchester and Front Royal was completely overwhelmed and their commander wounded. When the fighting ended, Jackson found he had lost less than 40 killed and wounded, while 700 Federal soldiers had been taken prisoner, along with two guns. The victory at Front Royal also enabled Jackson's men to claim possession of a veritable bounty of wagons and other supplies.

Upon learning what happened at Front Royal, Banks determined early on May 24 that he had no choice but to pull back to Winchester, and began evacuating Strasburg. When Jackson received word of this development around noon, he immediately sent out a flurry of orders for a pursuit. He ordered Ewell's command to advance directly on Winchester along the road connecting the town with Front Royal, while he took the rest of his command west toward the Valley Turnpike at Middletown in an effort to strike a decisive blow against Banks's retreating columns, which a band of Jackson's cavalry had begun stabbing at.

Rain and hail during the morning, as well as an efficient Union delaying force, greatly hindered the Confederate cross-country march to Middletown, and Jackson did not personally arrive in the area until midafternoon. Nonetheless, upon doing so Jackson was able to clearly see Federal supply wagons moving north slowly along the turnpike. He immediately called up some artillery to fire on them from high ground east of Middletown, which produced what Jackson later described as "a most appalling spectacle of carnage and destruction." Federal cavalry escorting the wagons quickly dispersed in confusion, and Jackson's men were able to swiftly grab 200 prisoners.

At around 4:00 P.M., Jackson had a message sent to Ewell informing him: "The enemy has retreated en masse toward Winchester. Major-General Jackson requests that you will move on Winchester with all the force you have left as promptly as possible. He will follow in force in the enemy's rear. . . . Hot skirmish just concluded here, with many horses and prisoners taken from enemy's rear guard." Shortly thereafter, however, Jackson countermanded the order. He directed Ewell to hold his command where it was in line with the forces around Middletown and ordered them to push south toward Strasburg in hopes that the bulk of Banks's command was still to the south. By the time Jackson learned that most of Banks's command was in fact to the north and is-sued orders for his men to reverse their march and head instead in that direction, some of his men had gone as far south as Cedar Creek. By 5:45 P.M., Jackson had also issued orders to Ewell to once again move his command in the direction of Winchester.

Despite the earlier miscues, the Confederate commander was still hopeful, he later declared, that even "if Banks reached Winchester, it would be without a train, if not without an army." Unfortunately for Jackson, after passing through Middletown, he found the Federals had left behind a massive quantity of supplies along the road, which Ashby's cavalry broke ranks to loot. An enraged Jackson continued to push his men north, but the cavalry's conduct and his own misjudgments dur-ing the afternoon had effectively eliminated whatever hopes he had of catching a major portion of Banks's army before night fell. Nonethe-less, he ordered his exhausted and hungry men to keep moving through the night toward Winchester. When a brigade commander expressed concern about his weary men, Jackson replied, "I yield to no man in my sympathy for the gallant men under my command; but I am obliged to sweat them tonight, that I may save their blood tomorrow."

Finally, Jackson had to bow to the needs of his men and halted them about two miles outside Winchester. They were only allowed a few hours' rest, though, for Jackson was eager to strike at Banks as soon as he could. At around 4:00 A.M., Jackson roused his men and ordered them back on the march. A message was then sent east to Ewell directing him to attack "at daylight."

Ewell, whose command had reached the point where the road linking Winchester and Front Royal crossed Buffalo Lick Run, promptly deployed his command astride the road and ordered an advance against the units holding the left of the Federal defensive line outside Winchester. As he did so, Jackson ordered an advance along the Valley Turnpike by the Stonewall Brigade. The Confederates quickly drove the Federals from their advanced positions, but they encountered difficulty when Federals posted along Abrams Creek began sniping effectively at the Confederate artillery support.

As Jackson's advance bogged down into an artillery duel, Banks attempted to shift some of the approximately 4,000 men in his command to the right. Jackson responded by ordering Taylor's entire brigade and part of Brig. Gen. William B. Taliaferro's brigade. They not only succeeded in thwarting Banks's move, but quickly drove the Federals from Bower's Hill, then pushed forward to crush the Union right flank. Meanwhile, Ewell moved a brigade to a position that menaced Banks's left and rear. Facing a Confederate force that outnumbered him by more than two to one and with both of his flanks collapsing, by 9:00 A.M., Banks had no choice but to order a retreat, having lost over 2,000 casualties to Jackson's approximately 400.

As he triumphantly reclaimed possession of Winchester for the Confederacy, the town's residents joyfully greeted Jackson with cheers. "The people seemed nearly frantic with joy," Jackson informed his wife afterward, "indeed it would be almost impossible to describe their manifestations of rejoicing and gratitude. Our entrance into Winchester was one of the most stirring scenes of my life."

Nonetheless, as he soaked in the cheers and reunited his and Ewell's command, Jackson was far from content. He wanted Banks's command pursued until it was completely destroyed. "Order the whole army," he commanded his staff, "to press on to the Potomac!" Upon personally clearing the northern outskirts of Winchester, Jackson caught sight of the broken remnants of Banks's beaten command streaming north. Wagons and equipment discarded by the fleeing Federals could be seen all along the turnpike. Jackson attempted to locate his cavalry so they could harass the beaten enemy, but no one could find Ashby or his men. Consequently, Jackson found himself compelled to push his exhausted infantry north.

Although they had enough energy to cheer Jackson as he pushed them forward, there was little left beyond that after the hard marching and fighting of the last week. Jackson was compelled to halt his march that day with Banks still out of his reach. His fury toward Ashby and his cavalry for its performance that day was still evident several months later, when he declared in a report that "Had the cavalry played its part in this pursuit as well as the four companies had done under Colonel Flournoy two days before at Front Royal, but a small portion of Banks's army would have made its escape to the Potomac." "Ashby never had his equal in a charge," Jackson would lament while discussing the episode several months later, "but he never had his men in hand. . . . He was too kind hearted to be a good disciplinarian."

As it was, 3,000 Federals had already fallen into Confederate hands, along with the massive supply depots at Front Royal and Winchester. Jackson's men claimed possession of nearly 10,000 small arms, along with half a million rounds of ammunition, as well as over 14,000 pounds of bacon, three tons of hardtack, over a ton of sugar, and more than $250,000 worth of medical supplies. Jackson's men soon came to refer to the man who was marching his command toward the Potomac as fast as he could that afternoon as "Commissary Banks."

Jackson's victories at Front Royal and Winchester also served to once again arouse alarm in Washington over the situation in the Shenandoah Valley and once again led them to compromise operations against Richmond. Lincoln, over the vehement objections of both McDowell and McClellan, ordered the former to suspend his march to McClellan, execution of which would have doomed the Confederate capital to certain capture. Instead, he directed McDowell to send Shields and two divisions east back to the Valley. If Shields's command could reach the Valley from the east and Fremont's command could do so from the west while Jackson was so far north, they would place themselves in Jackson's rear and cut him off. Thus, in addition to allaying his concern over Banks's force, Lincoln also thought this move would enable Federal arms to take advantage of an opportunity for decisive success in the Valley—albeit one that could only be pursued by compromising the far more important operations against Richmond.

Meanwhile, Jackson continued advancing down the Valley toward Harpers Ferry, while his quartermasters went to work moving the bounty of Federal supplies they had seized southward. At Charlestown on May 28, Winder's Stonewall Brigade swept aside a small Federal force with such ease that it aroused hopes in Jackson that he might have an opportunity to drive the 7,000-man Federal garrison at Harpers Ferry across the Potomac.

The following day, though, Jackson received word from Ashby that Fremont's force was then moving on Strasburg from the west. Nonetheless, on May 30, Jackson had his forces at the outskirts of Harpers Ferry and engaged in an artillery duel with the Federal garrison. His fading hopes that he could do more were completely extinguished, though, when reports arrived during the morning that the Federals were reinforcing Harpers Ferry and that Fremont's and Shields's commands were at that moment moving to cut his rear. By the end of the day Jackson concluded he had no choice but to order his command to pull back toward Winchester.

As Jackson rode in a car of the Winchester and Potomac Railroad ahead of his troops, a courier raced up to the train and persuaded it to stop. He then handed a message to Jackson reporting that elements from Shields's command had reached Front Royal and routed the small force Jackson had left behind to garrison the town (in the process they also reclaimed a good chunk of the spoils Jackson's men had captured a few days earlier). This placed the Federals nearly 10 miles closer to Strasburg than Jackson personally and far closer than the rest of his command, some of whom were still just outside Harpers Ferry.

Jackson immediately went to work. From his headquarters a flurry of staff officers emerged throughout the rest of the day and into the night, carrying orders to the various elements of his command to move south as fast as they could. Fortunately, Banks and the troops at Harpers Ferry were content merely to hold their position, which allowed Jackson's men to begin moving south without having to worry about their rear. Still, it was an exceedingly anxious time for Jackson. One staff officer later recalled that during this time Jackson "manifested more anxiety about getting the Stonewall Brigade back . . . than I ever saw him do at any other time."

Yet, as he led his command out of Winchester on the morning of May 31, Jackson's ability to maintain his composure had a soothing effect on his subordinates. "We left our friends in Winchester trembling for our fate & more than we trembled ourselves," one officer later recalled, "Everybody felt the danger, but everybody also looked at Old Jack & seeing him calm & cool as if nothing was the matter, they came to the conclusion that their destruction could not be as inevitable as they supposed."

Fortunately for Jackson and his men, they were blessed with good marching weather and a clear road as they pushed south along the Valley Turnpike. Fremont's and Shields's commands were not so fortunate and thus were compelled to advance cautiously, enabling Jackson to end his march just north of Strasburg on May 31, with his line of escape still blessedly open. The next morning, part of Fremont's command approached from the west, but Ewell and Ashby were able to block its advance all day long, giving the Stonewall Brigade time to catch up with the rest of Jackson's command after a 35-mile march through the rain. After giving them a few hours to rest, late in the afternoon Jackson ordered his entire force to resume the march south. They quickly cleared Strasburg and by the end of the day had reached Woodstock. They had also, as one soldier colorfully put it, "slipped through the jaws of the closing vice like a greased rat." "I did not fall back too soon," Jackson informed his superiors on June 2, "had I not been in Strasburg yesterday the Federals would have been." "Disgraceful," was how one Federal officer later described the whole affair, "I am utterly humiliated to have been mixed up in it."

While Jackson had foiled Lincoln's scheme to trap his forces north of Massanutten Mountain, Jackson and his command were not out of danger yet. If Fremont could hold the Confederates east of Massanutten Mountain, there was still the danger that Shields would move down the Luray Valley to the southern end of the mountain and get in Jackson's rear there. Jackson had no choice but to continue to push south. As Jackson's men marched up the Shenandoah Valley, Fremont pursued, but his efforts were frustrated by Ashby's cavalry, which performed its role as rear guard superbly. To the east, Shields's efforts were hampered by heavy rains and difficulty keeping up his supply trains.

CROSS KEYS AND PORT REPUBLIC

Meanwhile, Jackson consulted his maps and came to the conclusion that the village of Port Republic, where the North River and South River came together to form the South Fork of the Shenandoah River, was where his army needed to be. By the time night fell on a rainy June 5, the head of his command had nearly reached Port Republic after a tough march from Harrisonburg. That night, Jackson received intelligence indicating that Shields and Fremont were still widely separated and perceived that he had a window of opportunity for fighting each separately, if he chose to do so.

The following day, as his command settled into Port Republic, Jackson chose a handsome structure known as Madison Hall, located just outside the village, as his headquarters. Both he and his command were exhausted and, with a message arriving from Richmond stating that the Valley army could not expect reinforcements anytime soon, Jackson undoubtedly hoped he would have a few days to rest. But during the evening, word arrived that the vanguard of Fremont's command had caught up with the Confederate rear guard on Chestnut Hill just east of Harrisonburg. Although the Confederates were able to fight off the Federal attacks, Ashby had been killed, news of which reached a shocked Jackson that night. When the cavalryman's body was brought to Port Republic he made little effort to conceal his grief.

Jackson did not, however, let the loss of Ashby distract him from the serious problem he faced at the moment. The Federals were menacing his command from two directions. To deal with Fremont, on June 6 Jackson had posted the bulk of his command on the other side of the North River from Port Republic to watch the roads to Harrisonburg. Ewell's command held a forward position along Mill Creek at Cross Keys, while other elements from Jackson's command occupied high ground along the rivers overlooking Port Republic.

When June 8 opened, though, it was elements from Shields's command, specifically a mixed force of infantry, artillery, and cavalry commanded by Col. Samuel S. Carroll, that provided the first source of excitement. Carroll's command had been sent forward a few days earlier by Shields in an attempt to strike at Jackson's line of retreat. Carroll almost immediately identified Port Republic as his target. He arrived at the South River around dawn on June 8 and completely surprised the Confederates by pushing across the river and entering Port Republic. Carroll's force then penetrated deep enough into the town to get be- tween Madison Hall and the bridge over the North River that linked it with Jackson's command on the other side. Jackson, however, was able to elude capture and cross the North River to safety.

Despite the considerable confusion Carroll's bold move had created, and the loss of a number of staff officers who fell into Union hands, Jackson was able to organize an effective response that drove the Fed- erals from Port Republic. Efforts to maintain the momentum of the counterattack by a vigorous pursuit were cut short, though, a few miles outside Port Republic when the Confederates caught sight of more of Shields's command approaching. Jackson responded by ordering up 10 pieces of artillery, which effectively deterred the Federals from mak- ing a determined push toward Port Republic.

Meanwhile, to the north and west, at around 10:00 A.M., Fremont's command arrived in front of Ewell's position near Cross Keys. Jackson, understandably preoccupied with the situation in Port Republic and Shields's command, wisely left management of affairs at Cross Keys in Ewell's able hands. Although outnumbered significantly, Ewell had chosen his position behind Mill Creek well. He had a good field of fire in his front that effectively killed any hopes Fremont might have had of making a successful frontal assault. Within a half hour after the Feder- als arrived, both sides were exchanging artillery fire as Fremont began maneuvering his forces with an eye on attacking the Confederate right east of the Port Republic Road. The infantry on that part of Ewell's line responded effectively to this move and not only repelled the Federal offensive but drove the enemy back with a spirited counterattack. By the late afternoon, whatever aggressiveness Fremont had possessed at the beginning of the day had dissipated, and Ewell clearly had the situ- ation well in hand.

In Port Republic, Jackson began planning for the following day. After the repulse of Carroll's foray, he had shifted Winder's and Talia- ferro's brigades to positions from which they could monitor Shields's movements. He called Ewell to headquarters that evening and, after receiving a report on the fight at Cross Keys, directed him to leave a reinforced brigade at Cross Keys under the command of Brig. Gen. Isaac Trimble to watch Fremont, and bring the rest of his command south of the rivers to join in an attack on Shields on June 9. Evidently impressed with the boldness of the plan on top of all that had occurred in just the past few weeks, Ewell remarked to an officer as he left Jackson's headquarters, "do you remember my conversation with you at Conrad's Store when I called this old man an old woman? Well, I take it all back! I will never prejudge another man. Old Jackson's no fool."

Still, Jackson was taking an incredible risk in hoping that Trimble's force would be able to hold off Fremont long enough to allow him to deal with Shields. Recognizing time was of the essence, Jackson had his men on the move early on June 9. Nonetheless, he was confident. "By 10 o'clock," he assured one man, "we shall get them on the run." At around 7:00 A.M., they began arriving in front of a strong Federal position astride the road linking Port Republic and Luray. Dominating the Federal position was a piece of high ground on the Federal left known as the Lewiston Coaling. Leading the units from Shields's command that held the Federal line was the same Erastus Tyler (now a brigadier general) who caused so much trouble for Jackson in the fight at Kernstown that had opened the great campaign for the Valley so miserably for the Confederacy in March.

Despite the strength of the Federal position, Jackson threw his lead brigade, the Stonewall Brigade, at it as soon as it reached the field. Federal artillery and infantry brutally repulsed the attack. As Brig. Gen. Richard Taylor's brigade of Louisianans reached the field, Jackson ordered one of his staff officers to lead it to a position from which it could attack the Federal artillery position on the Coaling. Meanwhile, Winder's men took such a pounding in their uneven contest with Tyler's command that they began to waver. Seeing what was happening, Jackson rode up and personally pushed his men back to their original line, shouting, "The 'Stonewall' brigade never retreats; follow me!" Nonetheless, at one point the situation appeared so dire for Jackson's men that the Federal commander began making preparations for a counterattack. Before Tyler's men could execute it, though, Taylor's men went into action against the Coaling. Even though he had to make his advance over heavily wooded and broken ground, Taylor managed to overrun the Federal artillery position after a bitter hand-to-hand fight. Not only did this kill Tyler's hopes to launch a counterattack, but shortly thereafter Jackson had gotten enough troops up to Winder's position that the Confederates now enjoyed numerical superiority. He then ordered a general advance that forced Tyler to abandon the field.

After personally leading a brief pursuit that netted over 400 prisoners, Jackson pulled his command back to Port Republic. There he found an advance by Fremont's command had compelled Trimble's force to fall back across the rivers and had reached the high ground overlooking the river and Port Republic. From there, they fired their artillery at the Confederates, but with little effect. Even though Jackson, after reuniting his command, had no choice but to withdraw his command from Port Republic to Mt. Vernon Furnace near Brown's Gap in the Blue Ridge that evening, there was no question who had won at Cross Keys and Port Republic. At a cost of around 1,100 casualties, Jackson's command had inflicted over 1,600 on the Federals and captured six pieces of artillery. On June 10 Fremont's and Shields's commands fell back down the Shenandoah and Luray Valleys. Fremont's would not halt until they reached Mount Jackson after a decidedly dispiriting 36-mile retreat from Port Republic. "We have too many Maj. Genls," one exasperated Ohioan tartly remarked afterward, "too little brains."

Chapter 7

THE BATTLES FOR RICHMOND

GAINES' MILL

After enduring hundreds of miles of hard marching and fighting in the course of the remarkable campaign they had just brought to a triumphant conclusion in the Shenandoah Valley, Jackson and his exhausted men could be forgiven if they believed they were entitled to a substantial period of rest and refitting in June 1862. Unfortunately, the situation in front of Richmond would not permit this. To be sure, Jackson had, with considerable assistance from the authorities in Washington, succeeded admirably in his mission of inducing the Federals to reduce the pressure against Richmond. Yet, there remained the possibility that, if given time to breathe, Federal authorities in Washington might actually get their act together and reinforce McClellan to the point that the fall of the Confederate capital would be almost assured.

Robert E. Lee, who had been appointed to command the Confederate forces around Richmond after Johnston's wounding at the May 31–June 1 Battle of Seven Pines (Fair Oaks), knew he needed to act. He also recognized that as long as McDowell remained around Fredericksburg and McClellan was east of Richmond, the latter's army

In 1914 the Confederate Memorial Association commissioned French artist Charles Hoffbauer to produce a series of grand works to be displayed in the Battle Abbey in Richmond. Unveiled seven years later, Hoffbauer's Four Seasons of the Confederacy *immediately attained iconic status. Here, in the "Spring Mural," Jackson watches as his proud and battle-tested men pass in review during the great 1862 campaigns in the Shenandoah Valley and elsewhere that made him a legend. (Virginia Historical Society, 2005.340.A)*

was vulnerable to a turning movement against its long railroad supply line. Consequently, within a week of Jackson's victory at Port Republic, Lee decided he wanted Jackson's force at Richmond.

After receiving a note from Lee directing him to bring his command to Richmond, Jackson put it in motion on June 17. He divided his forces up and had them take multiple routes to confuse the Federals as to what he was doing. The following day, Jackson personally reached Staunton and boarded a train with his staff that took him to Waynesboro, where he rendezvoused with the rest of his command late in the afternoon. Jackson and some members of his staff then rode up to the top of the Blue Ridge. "The whole western slope of the mountain on both sides of the road," one member of the party wrote, "was covered with troops with camp fires burning. It was a very fine sight. . . . I said, 'General, I fear we will not find our wagons tonight.' He replied, earnestly, 'Never take counsel of your fears.'"

The following day, Jackson's men began moving toward Gordonsville on the Virginia Central Railroad, where they boarded the railroad
cars that were to take them to Richmond. By June 21, the vanguard
of Jackson's command had reached Gordonsville, where Jackson and
his staff were arranging for their trip. After investigating a false report
that a considerable Federal force had reached a point less than 20 miles
from Gordonsville, Jackson boarded a railroad car and traveled about
20 miles to Fredericks Hall. There he disembarked and mounted a
horse. He then rode for 14 hours straight, covering a little over 50 miles
to reach the Widow Dabbs house just east of Richmond, where Lee had
made his headquarters.

Upon arriving at the Dabbs house at midafternoon on June 23,
Jackson dismounted and soon thereafter was greeted by brother-in-law
Maj. Gen. Daniel H. Hill. The two officers were then called to Lee's office to discuss the situation. Two other generals, Maj. Gen. James
Longstreet and Maj. Gen. Ambrose Powell Hill, arrived shortly
thereafter. Lee then laid out for his subordinates his plan to take the
offensive against McClellan's army. Jackson learned his command
was to maneuver around the open northern flank of the Federal army
to attack the York River Railroad, which was then serving as Mc-
Clellan's supply line. This, Lee believed, would compel McClellan to
abandon his entrenchments and create an opportunity to strike a decisive blow at the Federals as they scrambled to protect their supply line.

After presenting his plan, Lee left and turned over to his subordinates the task of working out the details of how they would execute
the plan. June 26 was set for the start of the offensive, and as night
fell Jackson departed and rode 40 miles north and west to Beaver Dam
Station. He arrived at the station late on June 24 after a rough ride
through the rain, during which the exhausted general managed only a
few winks of sleep. He found the lead elements of his command arriving at the station with over 30 miles separating them from where Lee
wanted them to be in two days.

Nonetheless, Jackson decided to wait for his entire force to reach
Beaver Dam Station and turned the task of overseeing preparations for
their next move to his staff. With these tasks completed, Jackson put
his men on the march early on a blazing hot June 25 in an attempt to
meet Lee's directive for where he needed to be in order to carry out his
designated role in the offensive. Jackson's men covered 20 miles that

day, but were still 6 miles short of where Lee wanted them to be when night fell, although Jackson promised in a note to Lee that he would have his men on the march early on the 26th to make up the distance. Shortly thereafter, he received a message from Lee clarifying the commanding general's intentions for where he wanted Jackson's men to move, but without an adequate map of the area.

Consequently, Jackson had a hard time figuring out exactly what he was supposed to do. Then, to make matters worse, Jackson was unable to get his men on the march on June 26 until nearly six hours had passed after the time he had previously promised Lee. By noon they were still not where they were supposed to be according to Lee's plan. A little over four hours later, Jackson personally reached a rural crossroads known as Hundley's Corner. There he was expected to make contact with the rest of Lee's command in preparation for the decisive move against McClellan. Unfortunately for the Confederacy, the effort to reach that point left neither Jackson nor his tardy command in condition to do anything truly productive when they arrived.

While Jackson and his men floundered in their effort to turn the Federal position north of the Chickahominy River, an impatient A. P. Hill decided to launch a series of assaults against the main Federal line posted behind Beaver Dam Creek. With Jackson in no position to cooperate, the Federals were able to easily handle Hill's command and bloodily repulsed the Confederate attacks.

Nonetheless, knowledge of Jackson's movements and correct divination of Lee's intentions led McClellan to conclude he could no longer maintain a line of operations based on the York River Railroad, and he would be better off shifting his line of supplies to the James River and moving the Army of the Potomac south to a position on that stream. To give his command time and space to complete preparations for this move, McClellan decided to leave the forces that had bloodily battered Hill's command on June 26 north of the Chickahominy, but pulled them back a few miles to a more defensible position near Gaines' Mill. This would place them closer to the rest of the Union army and eliminate the threat of an attack on their rear by Jackson's command.

When Jackson arose early on June 27, he directed his command to head toward a road junction known as Old Cold Harbor. By placing his command there, Jackson presumed he would finally achieve his goal of reaching the rear of the Federal force north of the Chickahominy. McClellan's decision to pull back his forces to Gaines Mill and give up the York River Railroad as his supply line, however, had negated the importance of Jackson's reaching Old Cold Harbor. Jackson did not know this as he rode ahead of his command early on June 27. After riding for three miles, Jackson reached Walnut Grove Church. There he found A. P. Hill, who informed him that the Federals had fallen back to Gaines' Mill. Shortly thereafter, Lee and his staff arrived on the scene. Though disappointed with Jackson's failure to accomplish more so far in the operations against McClellan's army, Lee remained hopeful that something decisive could be accomplished north of the Chickahominy. Consequently, he directed Jackson to continue his march to Old Cold Harbor and the York River Railroad and try to take up a position in the rear of the Federals north of the river. He would then hold his position to block the Federal retreat while Longstreet's and Hill's forces attacked them from the east.

Unbeknownst to Lee, McClellan had already given up on the York River Railroad, and Maj. Gen. Fitz John Porter, the commander of the segment of the Federal army north of the Chickahominy, was establishing a good defensive position near Gaines' Mill that effectively covered his route of escape across the river. Consequently, as Jackson left Lee at around 11:00 A.M., he was going out to execute a mission that had no real purpose.

When other elements of his command reached Porter's position at Gaines' Mill early in the afternoon, Lee launched a series of attacks that produced tremendous casualties for his army but failed to make a dent in the Federal position. Meanwhile, at around 3:00 in the afternoon, Jackson and the vanguard of his command reached Old Cold Harbor. There Jackson learned from a staff officer dispatched from Lee's headquarters that Lee now wanted him to participate in the attack on Porter's position at Gaines' Mill. Jackson complied as promptly as he could, although the fact that much of his command was still strung out on the road to Old Cold Harbor at the time meant it took about two hours for him to actually get his command moving toward the sound of the guns at Gaines' Mill.

When Jackson finally got his men on the field, Lee rode over to greet him and made no effort to conceal his relief at his arrival, for the

Confederate army had so far gotten the worst of it in their tangle with Porter's command. "That fire is heavy," he remarked to Jackson, "Do you think your men can stand it." "They can stand anything!" Jackson replied, "They can stand that!" Lee then instructed Jackson to prepare to put his men into the fight. Even though it was late in the day and he was suffering from severe sleep deprivation, Jackson immediately threw himself into the task.

At around 7:00 P.M., Lee finally completed preparations for an assault by his entire command against Gaines' Mill, with Jackson's command on the far left. Jackson's troops took a terrible pounding in the attack, but elsewhere a brigade of Texans managed to achieve a breakthrough against the Federal line. By the time they did, though, it was too late in the day to fully exploit the success. Porter pulled his men back and by the following morning had successfully withdrawn across the Chickahominy. He did so in compliance with orders, conceding defeat at Gaines' Mill, but understanding that his men had given Lee's army two terrific beatings and McClellan time to complete his preparations to move the Federal army to the James River.

When morning rose on June 28, Jackson added D. H. Hill's division to his command in accordance with directions from Lee's headquarters. At the same time, he detached Ewell's division to accompany Confederate cavalry commanded by Brig. Gen. Jeb Stuart as they pushed east along the left bank of the Chickahominy to cut the York River Railroad. While they managed to destroy a considerable amount of track and telegraph lines, they were able to do so because the Federals had given up on the York River Railroad and were at that moment moving south toward the James River. Lee and the rest of the Confederate high command did not discern this until nearly the entire day had passed, though; consequently, it was not until the morning of June 29 that they began making active plans to respond to this development.

Key to these plans was the fact that in order to reach the James River, the Federal army would have to move south along a limited road network and negotiate a potentially significant bottleneck where it had to cross White Oak Swamp. Lee discerned a possible opportunity. He ordered Jackson to reconstruct the Grapevine Bridge over the Chickahominy that the Federals had destroyed after crossing that stream, and then use it to press the Federals as they moved south toward the White

Oak Swamp crossing near the Glendale crossroads. Meanwhile, the rest of the Confederate army would move to positions from which they could take advantage of a series of roads radiating east from Richmond to hit the Federal column in the flank. If the two arms of the Confederate army could catch the Federals before they reached the James River, Lee hoped to effectively destroy a large portion of McClellan's army.

WHITE OAK SWAMP AND MALVERN HILL

Upon learning of his role in Lee's plans, Jackson immediately went to work on June 29 reconstructing not only Grapevine Bridge but, in order to speed up the crossing of the Chickahominy, another span over the river known as Alexander's Bridge. These tasks, however, were not completed until much of the afternoon had passed, during which Jackson personally crossed the river to find out what was happening. After doing so, he could clearly hear the sounds of battle a few miles away around Savage's Station on the York River Railroad. There a division commanded by Jackson's old commander in Mexico, Maj. Gen. John Magruder, was battling the Federals. As Jackson contemplated whether to do something to support Magruder's efforts, around 3:30 P.M., a message from Lee arrived that indicated the commanding general wanted Jackson to remain in a position from which he could ensure the security of the Chickahominy crossings. Jackson dutifully obeyed the order from headquarters and returned to the river crossings. By doing so, though, he ensured that Magruder's fight with the two rearmost Federal corps would add more names to the casualty lists but achieve little else.

That night it began raining heavily around midnight, which frustrated Jackson's efforts to catch some sleep. An hour later, he issued orders to his men to be ready to move south from the Chickahominy bridges at dawn. He then rode over to Magruder's headquarters to discuss matters and found that general distraught over the previous day's events. After consoling Magruder, Jackson continued working through the night. Jackson's understanding of what role he was to play on June 30 was greatly improved when Lee arrived at Magruder's command post and explained his intentions for the day. Jackson, Lee instructed, was to take his command and push south from the Chickahominy toward White Oak Swamp in pursuit of the Federal rear. Meanwhile, the rest of the Confederate army would maneuver in such a way that would enable them to attack the Federals from the west.

Jackson's march on June 30 carried his men first to Savage's Station, where they found mass quantities of abandoned Federal supplies and a hospital where the Federals had left around 2,500 ailing soldiers. Jackson's men immediately began gathering supplies as their commander wrote a hasty note to his wife. "An ever-kind Providence has greatly blessed our efforts and given us great reason for thankfulness," he informed her. "To-day the enemy is retreated down the Chickahominy towards the James River. Many prisoners are falling into our hands. . . . I had a wet bed last night, as the rain fell in torrents. I got up about midnight and haven't seen much rest since."

After finishing his note, Jackson put his men back on the road to White Oak Swamp. The brutal heat and humidity quickly began to further sap the energy and spirits of man and beast alike. About noon, Jackson managed to personally reach the location of the bridge that carried the road over the swamp. He found it burned and the artillery in his advance already in position overlooking the swamp. He could also see wagons from the Union rear guard moving south on the other side of the stream, which led him to immediately approve work that artillery commander Col. Stapleton Crutchfield had already begun, clearing the vegetation around the swamp to create clear fields of fire.

Shortly before 2:00 P.M., this was completed, and the 23 Confederate guns began firing across the creek. Jackson then ordered Col. Thomas T. Munford's cavalry regiment to cross White Oak Swamp and seize three guns the Federals had abandoned after coming under fire from Crutchfield's artillery. Munford's men managed to drive off Federal skirmishers still at the crossing and cross the swamp with Jackson and D.H. Hill personally accompanying them. Then, just as Jackson and Hill reached the other side of the swamp, they came under heavy Union artillery and infantry fire. Recognizing that the Federals in front of him were in much greater strength than had been anticipated, Jackson pulled back across the swamp as the men he had assigned the task of rebuilding the bridge were compelled to give up their work.

Jackson then sent Munford's cavalry downstream and an infantry brigade commanded by Brig. Gen. Ambrose Wright upstream to look for alternative crossings of the swamp. Meanwhile, Crutchfield continued to duel with the Federal artillery on the other side of the swamp. When a brigade commander finally managed to locate a crossing, he rushed over to Jackson's headquarters and reported his find, but found Jackson too exhausted to even acknowledge his report. After he departed, Jackson sat down under a large tree and fell asleep for about an hour. Meanwhile, a few miles away, Longstreet's and A. P. Hill's commands were making a series of vigorous assaults on the Federals at Glendale, which were bloodily repulsed.

When Jackson awoke, he was still exhausted and barely able to function. He managed to dine with his staff that evening, but fell asleep while eating. Upon awakening, he departed and headed for bed. "Now gentlemen," he told his staff in perhaps an embarrassed admission of his inability earlier to fight through his exhaustion or overcome the stiff resistance the Federals offered at White Oak Swamp, "let us at once to bed, and rise with the dawn, and see if tomorrow we cannot do *something*."

Having finally gotten some decent rest, Jackson was his usual alert and energetic self the morning of July 1, 1862. Finding that the Federals defending White Oak Swamp had departed, he ordered his men across and linked up with the rest of Lee's command south of Glendale. At Willis Church, he met with Lee and the rest of the Confederate high command to discuss the situation. The Federals had pulled back to a strong position on Malvern Hill, and Lee, desperate to prevent them from reaching the James, was eagerly seeking some way to attack them successfully. The strength of the Federal line on Malvern Hill, though, led D. H. Hill to express dismay at the notion of testing it. "If General McClellan is there in force," he declared, "we had better leave him alone."

Lee, however, was determined to take one more shot at the Federals if it were at all practicable. Because it had been relatively lightly engaged the previous day, Jackson's command would participate in the effort. After moving forward about a mile and a half from Willis Church, Jackson got his first sense of just how strong the Federal position was when his men were greeted with tremendous blasts of Union artillery fire. Nonetheless, Jackson dutifully deployed his command on the Confederate left during the late morning and began further investigating what was before him.

As Jackson did this, Longstreet advised Lee that if the Confederate artillery were properly deployed and utilized something might be done. Longstreet's confidence was badly misplaced. "These few guns," one subordinate warned Jackson upon learning Lee had decided to test Longstreet's idea, "will not be able to live in the field five minutes." "General," Jackson brusquely replied, "obey orders." "I always obey orders promptly," the officer shot back, "but do not obey these willingly." Sure enough, as soon as the Confederates got some artillery in position, an effort in which Jackson participated actively and directly, the Federals promptly unleashed an ungodly storm of shot and shell on them. At one point a shell fragment struck a horse in the head near Jackson's position. An officer later recalled then seeing "Three or four horses much frightened . . . struggling to get away from their riders—& Gen'l J[ackso]n's old sorrel partaking the general alarm dashed off, pulling him down on his hands & knees. Turner, Maj. Nelson & I ran to him, fearing he was hurt—but he had recovered his feet & his horse kept pulling him along. After 20 or 30 yards of this, he managed to stop it, mounted & at once rode to the rear."

With the Confederate artillery effectively neutralized, the infantry assaults on Malvern Hill proved an exercise in futility. Jackson dutifully ordered D. H. Hill's division to play its role in the attack, but it was so brutally repulsed that Hill would declare two years later that his "recollections of Malvern Hill are so unpleasant that I do not like to write about it." That night, having administered a severe beating to their foes in the last engagement of what became known as the Seven Days' Battles, the Federals pulled back to an encampment on the James River at Harrison's Landing.

Jackson wanted to pursue them aggressively, but heavy rain, McClellan's management of his army in the movement to Harrison's Landing, and the Federal high command's effectiveness in selecting and preparing its position there killed Lee's and Jackson's hopes that more could be accomplished that day and in the week that followed. Thus, on July 8, Jackson received orders to pull back to the Richmond defenses.

For all they had accomplished in the Shenandoah Valley and in front of Richmond, Lee and Jackson justly merited the profuse praise that came their way in the aftermath of the Seven Days. With a terrific assist from the Lincoln administration, they had prevented the fall of Richmond and provided an incalculably valuable boost to Confederate morale. Nonetheless, Lee and Jackson were far from completely satisfied in July 1862. Both men longed to carry the war north, away from the environs of Richmond. Thanks to Washington, they would get the chance to do so—and in spectacular fashion.

Chapter 8

WHO COULD NOT CONQUER?

CEDAR MOUNTAIN

In response to the beatings Jackson had recently administered to the various Federal commands in the Shenandoah Valley, Lincoln decided in late June 1862 to combine them into a single Army of Virginia under the command of Maj. Gen. John Pope. The president hoped Pope would use his new army to menace the critical Confederate rail junction at Gordonsville, which connected Richmond with the Shenandoah Valley, and distract the Confederates from operations on the York-James Peninsula. By July 13, Pope's operations and policies bringing the hard hand of war to civilians had generated such anxiety in Richmond that Lee decided to send Jackson north with two divisions to deal with Pope. The rest of Lee's command, left in front of Richmond to defend the capital against McClellan's army, would operate under Lee's direct supervision.

Late on July 13, Jackson and the 11,000 or so men under his command began moving toward Pope, whose army was then still concentrating in the vicinity of Culpeper Court House between the Rappahannock and Rapidan Rivers. On July 19, having learned that Pope had not yet begun active operations in the direction of Gordonsville, Jackson decided to move there and personally reached the town that day. After setting up his headquarters, Jackson took stock of his situation and instituted a strict program of drill and discipline as soon as his command arrived.

The fact that Pope's command outnumbered his own at least four to one weighed heavily on Jackson's mind. But as long as McClellan's command was on the James River, Lee dared not weaken much further the forces defending Richmond. Fortunately, the arrival of reinforcements from South Carolina in mid-July did allow Lee to augment Jackson's command with a large division commanded by A. P. Hill. In addition to Hill's force, Lee sent Jackson a blunt message during the last week of July: "I want Pope to be suppressed."

With the arrival of Hill's command during the first week of August, Jackson immediately began planning offensive action against Pope. This was interrupted, though, by the unwelcome task that came to Jackson of dealing with the court-martial case of Richard Garnett over that officer's performance at Kernstown in March. On August 5, Jackson proceeded to Liberty Mills, a few miles from Gordonsville, where Richmond had decided the case would be tried.

It did not go well for Jackson. Even though Garnett's former subordinates made clear in writing that they supported his actions at Kernstown, Jackson refused to back down from pressing his case. Then, when Jackson took the stand on August 6, Garnett conducted a cross-examination that placed Jackson and his take on what had happened in March in a decidedly bad light. Although a member of his staff offered a staunch defense of Jackson from the stand the following day, it must have come as a godsend for Jackson when news arrived that a significant portion of Pope's command was pushing south toward the Rapidan River.

Jackson immediately sent out orders to his three division commanders—Ewell, Winder, and A. P. Hill—to put their commands on the march north toward the Rapidan. After encamping during the night of August 7–8 at Orange Court House, Jackson ordered the march resumed through what proved to be the second in a series of brutally hot days. Jackson, however, had made a late change in the marching orders that was not fully communicated to all of his division commanders. This combined with the heat to make for a very poor march by Jackson's command on August 8 and a contentious meeting between Jackson and Hill, whose march had been the one most negatively affected by the mix-up in orders.

The following morning, Jackson put his men on the march early. Expecting to encounter no significant resistance until at least Culpeper Court House, Jackson pushed his men across the Rapidan River, hoping to reach the village that day. About four miles south of Culpeper, though, Ewell's command made contact with what he initially thought was just some Federal cavalry. After bringing up artillery, they discovered that a large Federal presence was in fact in front of them. Jackson immediately began riding forward to the front. En route, he received reports indicating that the Union force belonged to none other than his old adversary from the Shenandoah Valley, Nathaniel Banks. "Banks is in our front, and he is generally willing to fight," he declared to a member of his staff, "And he generally gets whipped."

Ewell's command made contact with the Federals near an eminence known locally as Slaughter Mountain, soon to become better known as Cedar Mountain. A brigade from Ewell's division commanded by Brig. Gen. Jubal Early then took up a position to the right of the road to Culpeper, with its right anchored on high ground near the north slope of the mountain facing toward the Federals, to which Jackson directed some artillery. As Winder's division arrived on the field, Jackson ordered it to take up a position on Early's left astride the road. Once this had been done, he planned for Early to advance against Banks's front, while Ewell's other brigades turned the Union left and Winder menaced their right. When Hill's division arrived, it would deliver the *coup de grace* to Banks's force.

Banks's command struck first, demonstrating that the earlier defeats in the Valley had done little to diminish their commander's willingness to fight. Shortly before 6:00 P.M., Banks's infantry launched assaults against Jackson's position. Ewell and Early were able to hold off the attack against the Confederate right, but on the left Winder's division, command of which had passed to Brig. Gen. William Taliaferro when Winder was mortally wounded, was hit so hard it quickly began to fall apart.

So serious was the situation that Jackson felt compelled to ride forward and, after failing to pull his rusted sword from its scabbard, snapped both free to wave them and a Confederate battle flag to rally the men while bullets flew all around him. "Jackson is with you!" he shouted, "Rally, men, remember Winder!" "With the 'Light of battle' shedding its radiance over him," one observer later exclaimed, "his whole person had changed. . . . The men would have followed him into the jaws of death itself." The men rallied, and a fierce fight, some of it hand-to-hand, with the Federals ensued.

Jackson then rode to the rear in search of Hill's command, which he quickly found and ordered into the battle. Their arrival on the field tipped the scales in Jackson's favor once and for all. Banks, recognizing this was the case, ordered his men to break off the fight as the sun set and pull back toward Culpeper. Jackson attempted to put together a vigorous pursuit, but his exhausted command was unable to catch up with the Federals before nightfall put an end to the effort. This, and news that another Union army corps had reached Culpeper to reinforce Banks, put an end to Jackson's effort to follow up his victory at Cedar Mountain.

After two days holding the field, during which Jackson informed Richmond that "God blessed our arms with another victory," he pulled his command back across the Rapidan River. The hard-won victory at Cedar Mountain had cost Jackson over 1,300 men killed, wounded, and missing, while inflicting nearly 2,400 casualties on Banks's command. It had also taken some of the starch out of Pope, who on reaching Culpeper immediately ordered his command to operate strictly on the defensive.

MARCHING AROUND POPE

Pope's abandonment of whatever thoughts he might have had of taking the offensive once his command was concentrated was only partially due to the thrashing Banks had suffered at Cedar Mountain. Pope also knew Washington had issued orders to McClellan's army to return to northern Virginia to combine with the Army of Virginia. Of course, by doing so, Washington had freed Lee to lead the rest of his command north to deal with Pope. This Lee decided to do as soon as evidence of McClellan's pending departure arrived. By August 14 Lee had reached Gordonsville to meet with Jackson. Together they then began planning what they would do when the other units of Lee's command, direction of which Lee had assigned to Maj. Gen. James Longstreet, arrived.

Lee quickly decided to attempt to turn Pope's army, which was still concentrated around Culpeper Court House, from the east. However, delays in the arrival of some of Longstreet's troops and Stuart's cavalry, and a Federal raid against Stuart's camp at Verdiersville on August 18 that netted documents laying out Lee's plan, foiled the Confederate commander's hopes. Pope promptly eliminated the danger to his command by evacuating Culpeper and pulling back across the Rappahannock River on August 19.

As soon as news of Pope's retreat reached Lee, he ordered a vigorous pursuit, but the Federals were too swift, and the positions they occupied on the north side of the Rappahannock too strong for the Confederates to achieve anything. By the night of August 20, the Confederates had reached the south bank of the Rappahannock with Jackson's wing of the Army of Northern Virginia (although technically still the commander of the Valley District, for all intents and purposes Jackson's command was officially part of Lee's army from this point forward) on the left and Longstreet's on the right.

As this was going on, Jackson decided on August 19 to deal with a growing problem of desertion in his command. Three soldiers had been convicted by court-martials earlier in the month and sentenced to death. When an officer and chaplain attempted to intervene on their behalf, Jackson sternly rebuked them. "Men who desert their comrades in war deserve to be shot," Jackson insisted, "And officers who intrude for them deserve to be hung." Late in the afternoon, the sentences were carried out.

This sanguinary duty did little to staunch Jackson's desire, shared by his commander, to find some way to get at Pope's command as soon as possible. Portions of McClellan's army were en route to link up with Pope, and the Confederate high command dearly hoped to make something happen before the two Federal commands were combined. Pope's withdrawal across the Rappahannock killed whatever prospects existed for moving downriver to turn the Federal left. Thus, Lee looked upstream and directed Jackson to find a suitable crossing beyond the Federal right flank and use it.

Jackson's first attempt to do so on August 21 was thwarted at Beverly's Ford. The following day, the Federals made a stab at Jackson's rear by crossing at Freeman's Ford, but were decisively repulsed by Isaac Trimble's brigade in a sharp engagement. Meanwhile, Jackson finally managed to find crossings near White Sulphur Springs beyond the Federal right and ordered Ewell to send a force of eight brigades across under Early's command. As rain began to fall, Ewell expressed concerns that it might cause the river to rise and trap Early on the other side. "Oh," Jackson replied, "it won't get up—& if it does, I'll take care of that."

Jackson's confidence was badly misplaced. Almost as soon as he spoke, the heavens opened and a torrential rain began falling over the Rappahannock Valley. The river quickly rose several feet, effectively isolating Early's force from the rest of Jackson's command. From his headquarters overlooking the river, Jackson anxiously monitored the situation, his frustration evident the following morning when he ordered the arrest of every regimental commander in the brigade encamped in the vicinity for allowing their men to steal fence rails for firewood.

As the sun finally began to shine through the morning of August 23, Jackson rode down into the river at the site of a damaged bridge. From that point, he watched as the river fell during the afternoon and supervised the work of his men as they built a bridge that was finally completed around 4:00 P.M. Fortunately, a lackluster Federal response to news of Early's isolation and that officer's skillful handling of his command, which Jackson warmly praised afterward, enabled the Confederates to escape the perilous situation Jackson had unwisely put them in. Finally, with completion of the bridge, Jackson ordered Early to recross the river, which he finished doing during the night just as the Federals finally appeared in force on the opposite bank.

The setback to this effort to turn Pope's right meant that an operational stalemate was preserved along the Rappahannock, a situation that worked to the benefit of the Federals, as it allowed more and more of McClellan's forces to link up with Pope. Fortunately for the Confederacy, during the night of August 22–23, Stuart's cavalry had conducted a highly successful raid against the Federal rear. Among their prizes were documents that gave the Confederate high command a good sense of Pope's situation and the disposition of his and

McClellan's forces. Upon digesting the information contained in these documents, on August 24 Lee called Jackson, Longstreet, and Stuart to his headquarters in the vicinity of the hamlet of Jeffersonton.

There Lee laid out a new, bold plan. Jackson, he proposed, would make another attempt to get around Pope's right. This time, however, he would make a much wider march to the north and west, then turn east to strike the Orange and Alexandria Railroad deep in the Federal rear. This would enable Jackson to cut Pope's supply lines and communications with Washington, as well as a route over which reinforcements were being sent to Pope's army. This would probably compel the Federal commander to leave the strong position behind the Rappahannock that had so frustrated the Confederate high command and possibly render himself vulnerable to a decisive blow. Longstreet's wing, accompanied by Lee himself, would follow Jackson's route to be on hand when the time came to strike. The boldness of the plan and its promise of ending the stalemate along the Rappahannock in favor of a campaign of rapid maneuver naturally appealed to Jackson. He immediately and enthusiastically approved the plan. When Lee closed the council by asking when he could start the decided-upon movement, Jackson earnestly replied, "I will be moving within an hour."

Jackson was a tad overoptimistic in his response but nonetheless got his command on the march the following morning with commendable alacrity. Ewell's division would lead the march, followed by A. P. Hill's and Taliaferro's. The guide for Jackson's approximately 23,500 men was staff officer J. Keith Boswell, who knew the area well—in part due to his relationship with a young lady who lived nearby.

At 3:00 A.M., the great march began. Jackson's men first moved north through Amissville, then turned northeast to cross Hedgeman's River. After passing through Orleans during the afternoon they continued moving north until they reached Salem on the Manassas Gap Railroad—the same road Jackson's brigade had taken a little over a year earlier to reach the battlefield of First Manassas. As the head of Ewell's division approached Salem in the last stages of a 26-mile march, Jackson rode his horse to the top of a rise by the side of the road. Almost as soon as he did so, loud cheers rose up from among the men. Although manifestly gratified at the sentiment behind the troops' action, Jackson was even more anxious to do all he could to preserve the security of the march. Thus, he signaled to them to be quiet. The soldiers promptly obeyed and instead raised their caps in silent tribute as they marched past him. "Who could not conquer," Jackson warmly asked his staff, "with such troops as these?"

The following morning, Jackson once again had his men on the road early, moving east along the railroad toward the Bull Run Mountains and its pass at Thoroughfare Gap (which due to confusion in the Federal high command over what was happening had been left mercifully unguarded) en route to Gainesville. At around 3:00 in the afternoon, Stuart rode up to Jackson and reported for duty, having been sent, along with his cavalry, by Lee. Jackson promptly ordered Stuart to position his cavalry to cover the flanks of the marching column, which, upon reaching Gainesville, stopped moving along the railroad to Manassas Junction but instead turned right to follow the road to Bristoe Station on the Orange and Alexandria Railroad.

About a half-mile from Bristoe Station, Jackson halted his column and, while waiting for his entire command to arrive, took a brief nap. Before doing so, though, he ordered some of Stuart's cavalry to prepare to attack Bristoe Station and assigned a brigade from Ewell's command the task of providing infantry support. Shortly before night fell, the Confederates launched their attack, which quickly overwhelmed the small garrison of Federal troops guarding Bristoe Station.

As the Confederates claimed possession of the station, though, a train approached from the south. Jackson's men tried to derail it and, when that failed, stop it with small arms fire, but it managed to escape north to Manassas Junction. The Confederates then went to work a bit more thoroughly to prepare for the next train and were able to throw the next locomotive and many of its cars off the tracks. As Jackson's men began going through it, another train appeared and crashed into the remnants of the previous train still on the tracks. Shortly thereafter, a fourth train appeared from the north, but its alert engineer was able to stop short of the wreckage and throw his train into reverse fast enough to elude an effort by some of the Confederates to pursue it.

Shortly after the last train appeared, Jackson decided to let his tired men—who had just marched over 50 miles in two days—get some rest. Then, however, he received intelligence that the Federals had established a massive supply depot at Manassas Junction only seven miles away. Not wanting the Federals, alerted by the last engineer, to have time to begin removing the supplies, Jackson was delighted when Trimble showed up on the scene eager for action. Jackson immediately ordered Trimble to advance along the railroad to Manassas Junction. Trimble began moving out at around 9:00 P.M., and shortly thereafter was joined by Stuart's cavalry, which Jackson had dispatched to his aid.

Trimble's and Stuart's force reached Manassas Junction shortly after midnight. The Federals were almost completely unprepared for their appearance. Trimble and Stuart promptly attacked, quickly overran the hapless 300 or so defenders of Manassas Junction, and claimed possession of the junction. The following morning, Jackson ordered the rest of his command—minus Ewell, who received the unenviable task of defending the Confederate rear against Pope's army—to Manassas Junction.

Shortly after reaching the junction, Jackson looked out in the direction of Alexandria and caught sight of a force of about 1,200 Federals moving toward him. This force, commanded by Brig. Gen. George W. Taylor, had been dispatched from Alexandria when word reached Washington that a sizable Confederate force was on the Orange and Alexandria Railroad between the capital and Pope's army. Pope too, after a day of vainly trying to interpret the bits of evidence of Jackson's march that reached him, was then responding to Jackson's presence in his rear. Early on August 27, he ordered his command to leave the Rappahannock line. One wing of his army marched north and east via Warrenton toward Gainesville with the objective of reaching a position where they would to block Jackson's route of escape to the west. The rest of the Federal army would move north along the railroad directly toward Manassas Junction to hit the Confederates from that direction. Back in Alexandria and poised to follow Taylor's force in moving out toward Manassas Junction were several thousand more Federals.

Thus, for all the brilliance of his march around Pope, Jackson found himself in a potentially very dangerous situation on August 27. Fortunately for him, because Pope's efforts and those of the authorities of Washington were not coordinated, he would have the luxury of dealing with them separately. First, Jackson was able to lay an extremely well-conceived and executed ambush for Taylor's force. Shortly before 11:00 A.M., Jackson sprung his trap and so badly routed Taylor's command that it would inspire extreme caution in General McClellan, who upon his arrival at Alexandria had assumed responsibility for forwarding Federal troops there to the field.

With Taylor's command disposed of, Jackson's command took stock of what they had found at Manassas Junction. There were massive warehouses full of supplies, huge dumps of ammunition, and large stockpiles of medicine. Most appreciated by Jackson's famished men was the food they found in quantities and varieties the average Confederate could only dream about. In addition to staples of the soldier's diet like bread and bacon, Jackson's men found lobster salad, French mustard, oysters, and fine wine—although their commander did the best he could to keep the alcohol out of his men's reach. While Ewell's men kept vigil down at Bristoe Station, Taliaferro's and Hill's infantry, along with Stuart's cavalry, eagerly indulged themselves.

Still, Jackson never forgot that he was in hostile territory. News that Pope had forces moving toward Manassas Junction arrived during the afternoon from Ewell, who had taken up a defensive position behind Kettle Run. Fortunately for Jackson, Ewell skillfully managed his command and was able to fight off attacks by a Union division commanded by Brig. Gen. Joseph Hooker—the vanguard of Pope's army. Ewell's efforts ensured that when night fell on August 27, Jackson could rest assured that the soonest he would have to seriously deal with Pope would be the following morning.

SECOND MANASSAS

The fact that Pope's command significantly outnumbered his own, of course, made this something Jackson wished to avoid at that point in the campaign. Thus, that evening he ordered his men to grab what they could from the Federal stores at Manassas Junction, destroy the rest, and prepare for a night march. He ordered Taliaferro to move north along the road that connected Manassas Junction with Sudley Springs Ford over Bull Run. Hill and then Ewell would follow. Only Taliaferro's march went as planned, though. The guide Jackson assigned to Hill accidentally led it in the direction of Centreville. Meanwhile, Ewell's guide lost his way and further exhausted the tired men of that division by marching them back and forth before finally locating the rear of Hill's misguided command, which they then followed in the direction of Centreville. Finally, someone found Hill, and before long the Jackson's lost divisions were moving west along the Warrenton Turnpike to link up with Taliaferro near a small hamlet known as Groveton.

Jackson selected Groveton as the rendezvous point. He did so because less than a mile north of where the turnpike passed through the village there was a wooded ridge along which an unfinished railroad cut ran. In addition to providing a good defensive position, the ridge was conveniently close to Gainesville and Thoroughfare Gap, which Jackson knew Lee and the rest of the Army of Northern Virginia were then moving toward.

As Hill's and Ewell's men completed their march to Groveton, Jackson actively sought information on Pope's movements. One thing he wanted to prevent, if possible, was Pope pulling his army behind Bull Run. If he did so, that would place him close enough to Washington that the Federals could reinforce his army relatively easily and by doing so considerably lengthen the odds against Confederate success in the next major engagement.

By noon on August 28, Jackson had all of his men in position north of Groveton, with Hill's command on the left, Taliaferro's in the center, Ewell's on the right, and cavalry screening their flanks. Like the rest of his men, Jackson was exhausted from the past few days' exertions and, during the late morning, lay down for a nap.

Jackson was awoken by a messenger carrying a report that elements from Pope's army were then moving east along the Warrenton Turnpike toward Bull Run, a march that would place them in a magnificent position when they reached Groveton for a Confederate attack. Jackson ordered Ewell and Taliaferro to attack them. However, upon riding forward to the vicinity of the Brawner Farm, located a few hundred yards north of the turnpike, he learned that the Federals had turned south off the turnpike and were moving toward Manassas Junction rather than Bull Run. Jackson told Ewell and Taliaferro to halt to await further developments. His frustration at the passing of what seemed to be a golden opportunity was evident. "The expression of his face," one man later recalled, "was one of suppressed energy and reminded you of an explosive missile, an unlucky spark applied to which would blow you sky high."

On a more positive note, Jackson learned at midafternoon that the isolated condition of his command were about to end, as a courier informed him that Lee and Longstreet's commands were approaching Thoroughfare Gap and expected to pass through it the next day. Shortly thereafter, news arrived that a large Federal column was then moving east along the Warrenton Turnpike toward his position. An excited Jackson rode out to an open hill to confirm the information and to his delight saw that the report was true. After spending a few moments observing the Federal column, he then rode back to the woods in which his men were resting. After returning the salutes of his officers, he instructed, "Bring out your men, gentlemen."

The Federal force Jackson spied that afternoon consisted of a single division commanded by Brig. Gen. Rufus King, who was eating his supper when Jackson initiated what would become known as the Battle of Brawner Farm by ordering his artillery to open fire. The Federal column immediately halted, and one of King's brigade commanders, Brig. Gen. John Gibbon, rode forward to a rise just north of the Warrenton Turnpike east of Brawner Woods. There he spotted a Confederate battery and, thinking that was all that was in front of him, ordered a regiment from his brigade to move north under the cover of the woods to deal with it.

When the Federals reached the north edge of the woods, though, they were stunned to see a long line of Confederate infantry moving toward them. It was the Stonewall Brigade, which Taliaferro had sent forward. When they were less than a hundred yards apart the two lines halted and began furiously exchanging small arms fire. Gibbon ordered up the rest of his brigade, while Confederate calls for help led Ewell to commit two of his brigades to the fight. The Federal effort, however, was hampered by the fact that King had suffered an epileptic fit. Consequently, only Gibbon's brigade and two regiments from Brig. Gen. Abner Doubleday's brigade would be engaged. Despite the odds against them, Gibbon's and Doubleday's Federals held their ground in a brutal stand-up fight, in the course of which they inflicted a grisly wound on Ewell that would necessitate amputation of part of one of his legs and knock that invaluable officer out of action for several months. Finally, frustrated with what had developed into a stalemated battle, Jackson attempted to maneuver around Gibbon's left flank near the Brawner Farm. However, darkness and hard fighting by the Federals thwarted the attempt. That night, Gibbon and a still shaky King decided to abandon the field, but they had inflicted 1,200 casualties while suffering only 1,100 of their own.

If the tactical performance of the Confederates had left something to be desired on August 28, Jackson's decision to engage King's division did have the happy effect of driving from Pope's mind the notion that he would pull behind Bull Run the following day. Having finally found Jackson, and determined to fulfill his earlier hope that he might "bag" the wily Confederate's command, Pope ordered his army to concentrate in the vicinity of the old First Manassas battlefield so they could attack Jackson the following day.

Meanwhile, Jackson had to figure out who to replace Ewell and Taliaferro (who had also fallen wounded) with, choosing Brig. Gen. Alexander Lawton to take the former's command and Brig. Gen. William Starke to replace Taliaferro. Understandably anxious to find out where the rest of the Army of Northern Virginia was, Jackson also decided to ride out toward the Bull Run Mountains. After riding as far west from his own command as he deemed safe, Jackson desperately searched for any sign of Longstreet's location, even at one point putting his ear to the ground hoping to hear the sound of marching feet. "I shall never forget," the member of his staff who accompanied him that evening later wrote, "the sad look of the man that night as he gazed towards Thoroughfare Gap, wishing for Longstreet to come." Jackson then rode back to his command to anxiously wait for the morning.

Fortuitously, the early hours of August 29 passed without incident, which gave Jackson time to improve his position by pulling back his men to the unfinished railroad in a line extending from where Manassas-Sudley Road crossed Bull Run to the Brawner Farm. Cavalry covered his flanks, while about 40 cannon supported the line.

Finally, at around 10:00 A.M., the Federals opened fire with artillery on Jackson's position as a preliminary to an assault against Hill's division. Just as the Federals moved up to advance, though, Jackson received word that Longstreet's command had passed through Thoroughfare

Gap and was moving to take up a position on his right. The Federals then made a series of determined but not particularly well-managed assaults against Jackson's command that the Confederates were able to fend off in bitter fighting—some of it hand-to-hand. Then, in the late afternoon, the Federals gathered themselves for one last major assault against the left of Jackson's line. Hill, whose men had suffered terribly already in the course of the day, seemed to be barely hanging on. Jackson sent a staff officer over to Hill's section of the lines, who returned with a grim report on the situation and was then sent back to Hill. "Tell him," Jackson remarked, "if they attack him again, he can and must beat them." Jackson shortly thereafter made his way over to Hill's command post personally and received another grim report from Hill. "General," he replied, "your men have done nobly. I hope you will not be attacked again; but if you are, you will beat the enemy back."

Shortly thereafter, the Federals launched their attack. Relentlessly they pushed forward, driving Hill's command back. But then, just as they appeared to be on the verge of victory, a fresh brigade commanded by Jubal Early arrived on the scene, having been dispatched there by Jackson. With Early's arrival, the tide of battle turned and within a few moments it was the Federals who were being driven back. When a staff officer from Hill reached Jackson to report that the Federals had been repulsed, Jackson smiled and remarked, "Tell him I knew he would do it."

After night fell, Jackson received a summons from Lee to join him and Longstreet at his headquarters. Upon his arrival, Jackson found Lee gone and promptly lay down in a nearby tent for some badly needed sleep. When Lee returned, he ordered that Jackson not be disturbed and proceeded to plan for August 30 without him.

Jackson arose early that morning and, after a conversation with Lee, rode over to his command. From what he could see, he initially thought there might not be a fight that day, as the Federals did not seem to be planning on renewing their attacks. For his part, Lee had decided to wait and see if the Federals were going to attack and developed a vague plan for sending Jackson's command on another march around Pope's army if this did not happen.

Pope spent the morning of August 30 sifting through conflicting reports regarding the condition and intentions of the Confederate army.

Finally, he decided to accept those that coincided with his own belief that, after the battering it had endured the past few days, Jackson's command had to be in the process of retreating. Thus, shortly before noon, he ordered a pursuit. The pursuit ended almost as soon as it began when the Federals discovered Jackson's command was still holding the position it had so bitterly defended the day before. Deliberately oblivious to the fact that on August 29 Longstreet's command had gone into position south of Jackson's right and was then astride the Warrenton Turnpike, Pope decided to make one more attempt to crack Jackson's line.

At around 3:00 P.M., Pope launched a final assault by 12,000 men commanded by Maj. Gen. Fitz John Porter—the same man whose command had bloodily fought off similar assaults at Beaver Dam Creek and Malvern Hill only a short time before—against Jackson's line. Although some of Porter's men managed to reach Jackson's line and press it hard enough to compel some of the Confederates to resort to throwing rocks, his attack completely and utterly failed. The Stonewall Brigade in particular once again distinguished itself in the fighting, losing yet another commander, but gratifying their old one with their performance. Nonetheless, Jackson's command was hard pressed for a while, which induced Jackson to call for help from Longstreet. A portion of Longstreet's command, the artillery commanded by Col. Stephen D. Lee, was already contributing materially to Jackson's efforts by blasting Porter's flank. Longstreet, seeing an opportunity developing, was reluctant to send much more, preferring to retain as much as possible for a counterattack against Pope's command south of the Warrenton Turnpike.

Fortunately for Longstreet, as Porter's bloodied command began to fall back after the failure of their assaults, one of Pope's subordinates was so alarmed at the scale of Porter's defeat that he stripped the Federal position south of the Warrenton Turnpike of all but a single brigade—just as Longstreet's men began moving forward. Longstreet's command quickly overpowered the Federals south of the turnpike and surged forward to Chinn Ridge. There, and along the slopes of Henry Hill—the same Henry Hill where Jackson had stood "like a stone wall" 13 months earlier—the Federals managed to put up a stiff enough resistance to buy time for Pope to escape across Bull Run. Their effort was materially aided by the fact that Jackson, his command exhausted by the previous two days' fighting, did not move forward as vigorously as Longstreet's after Porter's repulse. Nonetheless, as night fell on August 30, the Federals were in full retreat back to Centreville. There was no question that the Confederate army had won yet another major victory at Manassas.

OX HILL

While almost any commander would have been content enough with the victory at Second Manassas to give his men an opportunity to recuperate from their exertions, this was not the case with Robert E. Lee or Stonewall Jackson. Moreover, they did not think the fact that Pope had managed to escape across Bull Run with his army largely intact meant the opportunity to achieve something even more decisive had passed. Thus, during the morning of August 31, Lee and Jackson crossed Bull Run to see what more might be accomplished. After drawing enemy fire that confirmed their sense that the Federals held Centreville in such strength as to make a direct assault impossible, they agreed to make another effort at maneuver. Jackson would take his wing of the army north along the Gum Springs Road to Little River Turnpike, then turn east and attempt to reach the point where it and the Warrenton Turnpike—Pope's main avenue of retreat to Washington—intersected just east of the small village of Germantown deep in the Federal rear. Longstreet's command would remain in front of Centreville long enough to hold Pope in place before following Jackson's route to Germantown.

As soon as he got back to his command and the task of getting to the men the first issue of rations they had received in three days was finished, Jackson put his men on the road as a heavy rain began to fall during the afternoon of August 31. The exhausted members of Jackson's command slogged 10 miles northward over muddy roads to reach Pleasant Valley Church on the Little River Turnpike by nightfall. A. P. Hill's lead division, however, had set such a rapid pace that it left stragglers all over the sides of the road. While Jackson certainly appreciated the virtues of a rapid march, he nonetheless deemed it necessary to take his subordinate to task.

After a rainy night, Jackson took the time to compose a brief note to his wife, informing her, "We were engaged with the enemy at and near Manassas Junction Tuesday and Wednesday, and again near the battle-field of Manassas on Thursday, Friday, and Saturday; in all of which God gave us the victory. May he ever be with us, and we ever be His devoted people, is my earnest prayer. It greatly encourages me to feel that so many of God's people are praying for that part of our force under our command."

Confederate hopes that they might successfully reach Pope's rear again took a significant blow shortly thereafter when Stuart reached Jackson's headquarters to report what he and his cavalry had found while riding east to see what was ahead on the turnpike. A strong line of Federal troops, Jackson learned, had been spotted a mile or two west of Germantown in a strong position astride the Little River Turnpike and behind Difficult Run. Jackson, however, still hoped that he could reach the Federal rear and ordered his men back on the road toward Germantown. Upon reaching the high ground where the turnpike intersected with Ox Road, known as Ox Hill, Jackson decided to halt his march to await the arrival of Lee and Longstreet's command. There he learned from Stuart that the Federals were still blocking the road to Germantown and responded by pushing forward a skirmish line toward Difficult Run to probe the Federal line. The Federals responded with such a heavy fire that Jackson called his men back to Ox Hill.

Meanwhile, on September 1 Pope had ordered his command to begin moving east along the Warrenton Turnpike toward Fairfax Court House. (It was elements of Pope's army, specifically the division commanded by Brig. Gen. Joseph Hooker, that Stuart and Jackson had encountered at Difficult Run.) Shortly after Jackson decided to halt and consolidate his position on Ox Hill, another segment of Pope's army began moving north from the Warrenton Turnpike along Ox Road with an eye on engaging the Confederates. Upon learning of this, Jackson promptly deployed his command facing south astride the Ox Road with Hill's division on the right, Lawton's in the center, and Starke's on the left.

Shortly thereafter, as a powerful thunderstorm began sweeping over the area, Hill's command made contact with an advancing Federal division. This touched off a fierce two-hour fight that came to be known as the Battle of Ox Hill (Chantilly). Neither side gained much of a tactical advantage in the battle, which ended with the Confederates holding their ground and two Union division commanders killed.

When Longstreet arrived on the scene, he smarmily remarked to Jackson, "General, your men don't appear to work well today." Even though it was true that the performance of his men on September 1 was not what it had been on other days, given what they had accomplished relative to what Longstreet's had over the past few months, Jackson certainly would have been justified had he cast aside diplomacy in responding to Longstreet's remark. Instead, he simply replied, "No, but I hope it will prove a victory in the morning."

When dawn rose on September 2, though, it quickly became clear that though the Confederates could claim a tactical victory at Ox Hill, the fight had effectively killed whatever faint hopes Lee and Jackson still had that they could cut Pope's army off from Washington. A quick pursuit and probe of the defenses of Washington soon confirmed for Lee and Jackson once and for all that they had run out of room for maneuver in Virginia. By the time night fell on September 2, 1862, Lee had already decided that the Army of Northern Virginia's next step would be to move north and cross the Potomac River into Maryland. Jackson heartily agreed.

Chapter 9

THE CAMPAIGN
IN MARYLAND

ACROSS THE POTOMAC

On September 3, Lee's army began moving north through Fairfax County toward the Potomac. As was now almost standard operating procedure in the Army of Northern Virginia, Jackson's three divisions led the way. Upon reaching Dranesville, Jackson, his mood soured by the fact that he had been compelled to ride another horse when Little Sorrell somehow went missing, called his three division commanders together. He directed them to synchronize their watches with his own and gave them specific directions for the next day—placing special emphasis on their following closely his now standard practice of alternating 50 minutes of marching with 10 of rest.

Jackson's subordinates did not follow his instructions as closely as he wanted on September 4, though, which further inflamed his already foul mood. He snapped at Brig. Gen. Maxcy Gregg when he found his command still in camp 30 minutes after Jackson had directed the march to begin. Jackson then interjected himself into the management of Col. Edward Thomas's brigade in a way that provoked Thomas's division commander, A. P. Hill, to thrust his sword toward Jackson and offer his resignation. Jackson responded by ordering Hill's arrest for dis-obedience of orders and placed Brig. Gen. Lawrence O'Bryan Branch in command of his division. Upon reaching Leesburg during the after-noon and establishing his headquarters just north of the town, Jackson ignored a request from Hill for documentation of the charges against him. He then, after talking with a native Marylander serving in the army in an effort to gain information about the state, rode back to Leesburg to discuss the situation with Lee.

On September 5, Jackson ordered his men toward the Potomac, following D. H. Hill's division, and crossed the river into Maryland at White's Ford. The men crossed with little difficulty, but Jackson's wagons had a more difficult time. Fortunately, Maj. John Harman was able to untangle the situation. However, in the process, he employed so much profanity that he anticipated a rebuke from Jackson, under whose personal observation he had done his work. Jackson, though, was satisfied when Harman explained, "There's only one language that will make mules understand on a hot day that they must get out of the water."

A less comic episode occurred the following day when Jackson led his command to Frederick, the principal town in the Monocacy River valley between South Mountain and Parr's Ridge. With Little Sor-rel's whereabouts still unknown, Jackson had accepted a replacement mount offered by a Maryland farmer the day before. The horse proved to be more than Jackson could handle. The first time he spurred it dur-ing the morning of September 6, it reared and fell back on the ground. It took a half hour afterward for a badly bruised Jackson to feel well enough to ride in an ambulance. By the time Frederick was reached, he was once again able to mount a horse and entered the town to a far from enthusiastic reception from its fiercely Unionist residents. "We do not appear," he remarked, "to have many friends here." Jackson then made headquarters on the Best Farm south and east of the town, near Lee's and Longstreet's command posts, and did the best he could to recuperate from his fall.

The following day, Jackson put his staff to work making maps and fending off A. P. Hill's demands for a formal copy of the charges filed against him. He also had to deal with complaints from local residents against some of his men for treating them in a way that was "bringing odium upon the army." Finally, that Sabbath evening, he was able to make his way to a church service at the Evangelical Reformed Church in Frederick. The reverend was an unwavering Unionist, who made no effort to conceal his sentiments. Jackson, however, missed this, for, as one observer later recalled, "As usual, he fell asleep, but this time more soundly than was his wont. His head sunk upon his breast, his cap dropped from his hands to the floor, the prayers of the congregation did not disturb him, and only the choir and the deep-toned organ awakened him. Afterward, I learned that the minister was credited with much loyalty and courage because he had prayed for the President of the United States in the very presence of Stonewall Jackson. Well, the general didn't hear the prayer."

HARPERS FERRY

By September 8 the army's time in and around Frederick was quickly coming to an end. Lee had decided that he could no longer rely on a line of communications and supply that ran through the Virginia Piedmont and would instead rely mainly on one that ran through the Shenandoah Valley. Union garrisons at Harpers Ferry and Martinsburg were situated way too close for comfort to such a line, but Lee surmised they could be eliminated before Federal forces around Washington would be ready for action. Thus, during the afternoon, Lee called Jackson to headquarters and described his plan for dealing with the Federals in the Shenandoah Valley.

On September 9, Special Orders No. 191 formally laid out Lee's plan. Jackson's three divisions would march west along the road to Hagerstown "and after passing Middletown, with such portion as he may select take the route toward Sharpsburg cross the Potomac at the most convenient point and by Friday morning [September 12] take possession of the Baltimore & Ohio Railroad, capture such of the enemy as may be at Martinsburg and intercept such as may attempt to escape from Harper's Ferry." Meanwhile, two divisions operating under the direction of Maj. Gen. Lafayette McLaws were to seize Elk Ridge and occupy its southern end, Maryland Heights, which overlooked the Potomac River and dominated Harpers Ferry. Another division, commanded by Brig. Gen. John Walker, was to cross the Potomac back into

Virginia, then seize Loudoun Heights, which overlooked the Shenandoah River and dominated Harpers Ferry from the south and east. While these operations were taking place, Longstreet's command would move to Hagerstown and leave D.H. Hill's independent division at Boonsboro, to watch Turner's Gap, where the National Turnpike provided the main crossing of South Mountain. Stuart's cavalry would remain east of South Mountain to screen the movement and keep an eye out for any Federals moving out of Washington.

On September 10, the operation began. As Jackson's 14,000 men moved west during the early morning hours, he conspicuously inquired from local residents about roads to Chambersburg, Pennsylvania, in an effort to disguise his actual route and sow confusion. After a march of about 15 miles that carried them over Catoctin Mountain, through the picturesque Middletown Valley, and over South Mountain at Turner's Gap, Jackson halted his command just outside of the town of Boonsboro.

As his men settled into their camps that afternoon, Jackson gave members of his staff permission to enter Boonsboro to visit friends. Shortly thereafter, Jackson decided to visit the town on his own. He was walking with his horse toward Boonsboro when he caught sight of some staff officers riding out of the town with tremendous haste. They had just encountered a force of Federal cavalry that had entered Boonsboro from the south, chased the Confederates in the town out, and could be seen riding toward Jackson. The general promptly mounted his horse and raced back to the safety of his own lines. The Federals, however, quickly broke off their pursuit and were soon gone. Nonetheless, this close shave undoubtedly contributed to Jackson's decision not to cross the Potomac at Sharpsburg, but to instead push further west to Williamsport and cross the river there—a decision that would add a considerable amount of time and distance to his movements. It all but ensured that Lee's expectation that the operation against Harpers Ferry could be wrapped up before the Federals could cause trouble from the direction of Washington would not be fulfilled.

Jackson did his best. On September 11, he pushed his command to Williamsport and crossed the Potomac at Light's Ford, then pushed another 7 miles in the direction of Martinsburg to complete a march of 20 miles for the day. By the time Jackson got his men on the road the following morning, though, the commander of the Union garrison at Martinsburg had evacuated the town and was moving to join his forces with those at Harpers Ferry. Jackson and his men occupied Martinsburg early on September 12 and received an enthusiastic welcome from its residents. Jackson especially attracted their attention, as did Little Sorrel, with whom the general had recently and happily been reunited.

Finally, at around noon on September 13, Jackson and his men reached Halltown, just west of Harpers Ferry. By then, McLaws's successful effort to wrest control of Maryland Heights from the Federals had just about been completed, while Walker's command was only a few hours away from securing possession of undefended Loudoun Heights. Jackson had his three divisions occupy Schoolhouse Ridge, located about a mile west of Bolivar Heights, where the bulk of the Federal force at Harpers Ferry was posted.

Although Jackson appreciated the virtues of celerity in his operations against Harpers Ferry, the position on Bolivar Heights was too strong to be attacked directly. Thus, he decided to make September 14 a day for artillery. By noon, Jackson had received word from Walker that he was ready to open fire on Harpers Ferry, while McLaws was still struggling to bring his artillery up.

Finally, during the afternoon, the Confederate bombardment commenced. The Federals were quickly demoralized by the experience of receiving fire from an enemy holding commanding ground and able to fire into them from three directions, but to the dismay of the Confederates they gave no sign of being ready to lay down their arms. Thus, Jackson ordered A. P. Hill (whom he had restored to command a few days earlier) to attempt to maneuver around the southern flank of the Federal position on Bolivar Heights. Hill quickly reached a position near the Murphy Farm, from where he could menace the flank of the Federals on the heights. That evening Jackson was able to inform Lee, "Through God's blessings the advance which commenced this evening, has been successful thus far, and I look to Him for complete success tomorrow. The advance has been directed to be resumed at dawn tomorrow morning."

The message reached Lee early on September 15. Unfortunately, by then Longstreet's and D. H. Hill's commands were in retreat toward the Potomac River after suffering a severe defeat at the hands of the

Federals at South Mountain. Jackson's note, however, in combination with success finding good defensive ground behind Antietam Creek, led Lee to reconsider leaving Maryland. Instead, he decided to halt in front of Sharpsburg during the morning of September 15 in hopes that Jackson could finish up the operation at Harpers Ferry in time to join the rest of the Confederate army there before the Federals could follow up their victory at South Mountain.

Jackson did not disappoint. The Confederate gunners resumed firing on Harpers Ferry early on September 15, and by 8:00 A.M., the town's defenders decided they had endured enough. Jackson asked their commander for unconditional surrender and received it. He then sent a message to Lee reporting, "Through God's blessing, Harpers Ferry and its garrison are to be surrendered. As Hill's troops have borne the heaviest part in the engagement, he will be left in command until the prisoners and public property shall be disposed of. . . . The other forces can move off this evening so soon as they get their rations." Jackson then wrote a short note to his wife. "[O]ur God has given us a brilliant victory at Harper's Ferry today," he exulted, "Our Heavenly Father blesses us exceedingly. I am thankful to say our loss was small."

The same could not be said of the Federals. Over 12,000 Union soldiers had been surrendered, along with over 12,000 weapons, hundreds of wagons and mules, and 73 pieces of artillery. Not until World War II would more U.S. soldiers fall prisoner to an enemy army.

As they formally went through the process of surrendering, the defenders of Harpers Ferry felt compelled to pay tribute to the man whose efforts had brought about their defeat. As a weary and roughly attired Jackson rode into Harpers Ferry from Bolivar Heights, one member of his command later recalled, "Almost the whole mass of prisoners broke over us, rushed to the road, threw up their hats, cheered, roared, bellowed. . . . The general gave a stiff acknowledgement of the compliment, pulled down his hat, drove spurs into his horse, and went clattering down the hill." One Union soldier called out upon catching a glimpse of Jackson, "Boys, he's not much for looks, but if we'd had him we wouldn't have been caught in this trap."

After briefly allowing his men to indulge in the spoils of their contest, Jackson issued orders putting them on the road to Sharpsburg. By midnight, he had personally begun his 17-mile trek to Sharpsburg, accompanied by Brig. Gen. John R. Jones's and Brig. Gen. Alexander Lawton's divisions. After crossing the Potomac at Boteler's Ford just down river from Shepherdstown, Jackson pushed on to Sharpsburg to meet up with Lee. During the afternoon of September 16, he met with Lee and Longstreet at the Jacob Grove house on Sharpsburg's town square to discuss Lee's plan, once the army was reconcentrated, to move north toward Hagerstown with Jackson's command leading the way.

As they were talking, though, news that the Federals had crossed Antietam Creek north of Sharpsburg and were poised to menace the road to Hagerstown led Lee and Jackson to give up any thoughts they had of leaving Sharpsburg and resign themselves to fighting a defensive battle there. Jackson then rode back to where he had let Jones and Lawton rest their commands after crossing the Potomac to move them into position on the Confederate left north of Sharpsburg.

ANTIETAM

There Jackson deployed his command to defend a plateau near the Dunker Church at the intersection of the Hagerstown and Smoketown roads. To defend the plateau, and the superb platform it provided for artillery, Jackson placed his two divisions in a line that extended from a patch of woods (later known as the West Woods) west of the Hagerstown Turnpike several hundred yards east to ground upon which a small cemetery was located. He posted Lawton's division east of the pike and Jones's west of it. When Lawton's command moved into position late on September 16 it relieved Brig. Gen. John Bell Hood's division, which had just fought a sharp skirmish with Federal forces in a stand of trees that came to be known as the East Woods, through which the Smoketown Road passed. This enabled Hood's command to go into reserve around the Dunker Church. That night a drizzling rain fell as both sides steeled themselves for what promised to be a tough fight the following day.

What would be the bloodiest single day in American military history began just as the sun began to rise on September 17. The commander of the Union Army of the Potomac, Maj. Gen. George McClellan, had sent two corps under the immediate command of Maj. Gen. Joseph Hooker across the Antietam to deal with the Confederates north of Sharpsburg. Hooker selected as his tactical objective the Dunker Church, where the Smoketown and Hagerstown roads connected, and ordered a division to follow each road south toward the church. After brutal, bitter fights in a 30-acre cornfield and the East Woods that left Jones's and Lawton's commands decimated, Hooker's command looked poised to achieve its tactical objective before the battle was two hours old. However, Jackson had already ordered Hood's division up from its reserve position. Hood then proceeded to launch a spirited—and vicious—counterattack that blunted the momentum of the Federal offensive but left his own command, as Hood later put it, "dead on the field."

Before the Federals could take advantage, units from D. H. Hill's division reached the Cornfield. They briefly stabilized the situation, but then a fresh Union division appeared on their flank and compelled Jackson to give up the fight for the Cornfield and East Woods, pull his badly battered command back to the cover of the West Woods, and concede the high ground in front of the Dunker Church to the Federals.

Then, at around 9:00 A.M., a new, powerful, and veteran Union corps began arriving on the field. Even before this development, Jackson had sent messages to Lee's headquarters requesting reinforcements. Lee responded as promptly as he could, but whether the additional units would arrive in time and be able to achieve anything was a decidedly open question.

Fortunately for Jackson, by this time in the battle Hooker had fallen wounded, and command of the Federal effort north of Sharpsburg had fallen into the hands of the much less able Maj. Gen. Edwin Sumner. Sumner then proceeded to order an advance from the East Woods toward the West Woods, thinking that a determined attack there might finish off the Confederate position north of Sharpsburg.

He may well have been proven correct, had not the reinforcements Lee dispatched to Jackson's aid arrived just as the Federals were moving into the West Woods, or had Sumner taken sufficient precautions to make sure his southern flank was not exposed. Instead, the stage was set for a Federal disaster. As elements from Jackson's command put up a dogged defense against Sumner's front at the western edge of the woods, Maj. Gen. Lafayette McLaws's division came up from the south and slammed into and around the Federal flank. Taking fire from three directions and with Sumner shouting "My God, we must get out of this," within 20 minutes the Federals were in full retreat, having lost around 40 percent of the men Sumner had led into the woods.

Part of McLaws's command unwisely attempted to follow up this success with an attack the Confederates hoped would drive the Federals from their foothold on the Dunker Church plateau. The Federals easily repulsed this series of poorly conceived Confederate attacks, then followed up their success by advancing into the West Woods. Once again, fortune smiled on Jackson, for the Federals that entered the woods lacked the ability to do much damage. Thus, as the battle shifted southward, they gave Jackson and his command a badly needed opportunity to recuperate from the brutal fighting that had taken place that morning.

By noon, whatever strain constantly being pushed to the brink of disaster that morning had inflicted on Jackson's nerves had clearly diminished. His spirits received a further boost when Hunter McGuire reached him with some peaches. Jackson happily accepted several and quickly devoured them. As he did so, an understandably anxious McGuire asked, "Can our line hold against another attack?" Jackson replied, "I think they have done their worst. There is now no danger of the line being broken."

Jackson was correct. But of course, neither he nor Lee were ever satisfied with merely holding their lines. As the Federal effort shifted from Jackson's front to the southern end of the field during the middle of the day, Lee hatched a scheme to take the offensive using the forces then operating under Jackson's command. He did so in part to escape a Federal battle plan that was squeezing the Army of Northern Virginia into a smaller and smaller box with only a single, vulnerable line of retreat across the Potomac. Jackson's infantry, Lee hoped, would press the Federals north of Sharpsburg, while Stuart's cavalry maneuvered around their flank. If successfully executed, such an operation might induce the Federals to pull back their right, clearing an escape route for Lee's army to Hagerstown.

Given how powerful the Federal forces were—especially in artillery—north of Sharpsburg, this was clearly a plan born of desperation. Nonetheless, Stuart and Jackson dutifully began exploring its feasibility.

Jackson rode over to the section of his line held by Brig. Gen. John Walker's division and asked one of its regimental commanders if he thought it would be possible to capture a nearby Federal artillery position. When the colonel replied that he thought it was too strongly supported by infantry for an attack to succeed, Jackson asked him, "Have you a good climber in your command?" When the colonel asked around, a private by the name of William Hood stepped forward and offered his services. Jackson promptly sent him up a nearby tree. When Hood reached the top, Jackson called out, "How many troops are over there?" Hood excitedly replied, "Oceans of them!" Seeking a bit more precise calculation, Jackson told Hood to count the number of regimental flags he could see. As Hood counted out loud, Jackson repeated each number. When Hood called out "39," Jackson put an end to the exercise. "That will do," he informed Hood, "Come down, sir."

Meanwhile, Stuart found it possible to maneuver his cavalry around the Federal left. Then, however, upon reaching a position beyond the Union flank, he foolishly decided to open fire with some of his artillery. The Federals responded by throwing back such a quantity of ordnance that they killed whatever faint hopes remained regarding the feasibility of Lee's plan to move north. Fortunately, the timely arrival shortly thereafter of A. P. Hill's command from Harpers Ferry thwarted the last major Federal offensive of the day south of Sharpsburg so that when night fell on September 17 the Army of Northern Virginia, though exhausted and badly bloodied, still held the field.

As the sun went down, Jackson made his way to army headquarters west of Sharpsburg. There he met with the rest of the army's high command and learned that, despite uniformly grim reports from every one of his subordinates, Lee had no intention of retreating across the Potomac that night. When they learned the news, neither Jackson nor any of the other officers in attendance objected.

Incredibly, despite having taken a savage beating the day before and the fact that his army was clearly—and badly—outnumbered, as the early morning hours passed on September 18, Lee again considered taking the offensive. He rode over to Jackson's command post near the Dunker Church and proposed that he take 50 pieces of artillery and smash the Union right. Jackson did not think this course of action held out much prospect of success and communicated this opinion effectively enough that Lee decided to send artillerist Col. Stephen D. Lee to Jackson to discuss the matter. When he reached Jackson, the general said only, "Colonel Lee, I wish you to take a ride with me."

Upon reaching the base of a hill, the two men dismounted and proceeded on foot to its crest. There Jackson instructed Lee to "take your glasses and carefully examine the Federal line of battle." Lee did so and saw no evidence that the Confederate army could accomplish anything more at Sharpsburg. "General," Col. Lee remarked, "that is a very strong position, and there is a large force there." "Yes," Jackson replied, "I wish you to take fifty pieces of artillery and crush that force, which is the Federal right. Can you do it?" Col. Lee said, "General, I can try. I can do it if anyone can." Jackson replied, "That is not what I asked you sir. If I give you fifty guns, can you crush the Federal right? . . . . I want your positive opinion, yes or no." After one more look through his field glasses, the colonel finally answered, "General, it cannot be done with fifty guns and the troops you have near here."

Jackson then returned with Col. Lee to the vicinity of the Dunker Church and sent the artillerist on to army headquarters. There the colonel told General Lee about his and Jackson's reconnaissance and what they had concluded about the feasibility of his plan for taking the offensive. With that, whatever hopes Lee had that he could stay in Maryland vanished. That night, the Army of Northern Virginia abandoned its lines and fell back toward Boteler's Ford just below Shepherdstown. At around 2:00 A.M., on September 19, Longstreet's wing of the army began crossing the Potomac; Jackson's command followed at around daylight and by 11:00 A.M., the last elements of the Army of Northern Virginia had finished crossing.

To cover the crossing, Lee had posted a strong force of artillery on the Virginia side of the river. Late in the afternoon, Federal infantry reached the river, where the two sides were vigorously exchanging artillery fire. Then, sensing a slackening of Confederate fire, Union general Fitz John Porter ordered some infantry to cross the river and see if they could accomplish anything. The suddenness with which the Federals rushed across the river took the Confederates by surprise and they were soon put to flight. Shortly thereafter, the officer Lee had left in charge at the ford was at headquarters reporting to Lee and Jackson that the army's entire Reserve Artillery had been captured.

Early the following morning, Jackson personally rode toward the river to find out what had happened. He found most of the artillery had not in fact been captured, but that the Federals seemed determined to follow up their success of the previous day. Fortuitously, Jackson had already ordered A. P. Hill's division to return to the ford to deal with Porter. Hill's men arrived on the scene around 9:00 A.M., and promptly assaulted a small force Porter had pushed across the river. Aided by the fact that many of Porter's men were carrying faulty weapons, Hill quickly drove the Federals back across the river, inflicting what Jackson later described as "an appalling scene of the destruction of human life." In the process, the Confederates recovered nearly all of the cannon lost the previous day and put an end to any thought the Federals might have had of following up their victory at Antietam with a vigorous pursuit across the Potomac.

Chapter 10

FREDERICKSBURG

FROM THE VALLEY TO THE RAPPAHANNOCK

After the Confederate victory at the Battle of Shepherdstown, Lee ordered Jackson to fall back along with the rest of the army up the Shenandoah Valley toward Winchester. At the small hamlet of Bunker Hill just north of Winchester, Jackson halted his command and ordered it to go into camp so the men could rest and recuperate from the Maryland Campaign. The rich bounty of the Shenandoah Valley enabled the men to eat well, while good weather did much to bolster spirits. Nonetheless, Jackson and Lee were determined to maintain strict discipline and watched their men closely, regularly inspecting their arms, conducting courts-martial, and cracking down quickly on men who deviated from the regulations. Among the measures Jackson took during this time to improve the efficiency of his command was to replace Andrew Jackson Grigsby, whose performance he found wanting, as commander of the Stonewall Brigade with Elisha F. "Bull" Paxton.

Jackson also decided to write to Gen. Lee on September 24 to ask that, in light of his exemplary conduct during the Maryland Campaign, the charges he had earlier leveled against A. P. Hill be dropped. Hill,

This photograph, taken in 1862 at Winchester, Virginia, is one of two taken of Jackson during the war and the one preferred by his wife, who thought it more effectively displayed "the beaming sunlight of his home-look." The woodcut on the right, which appeared in Battles and Leaders of the Civil War, *was based on this photograph. (Getty Images/Johnson, Robert Underwood and Clarence Clough Buel, eds.,* Battles and Leaders of the Civil War. *New York: The Century Co., 1887.)*

however, believed his personal honor has been insulted and would not accept anything less than complete exoneration, which could only come about if the charges were fully investigated. Consequently, Jackson had no choice but to continue to pursue the case. While Lee diplomatically endeavored to keep the matter open, and thus unresolved, Hill's course ensured that his relations with Jackson would remain frosty and strictly formal. Lee, for one, had no interest in encouraging anything that might be perceived as an attack on the man whose ability was unquestioned and accomplishments had made him a hero. "The soldiers cheer him as if they think him to possess some supernatural power," one proclaimed, "If Jesus Christ were to ride along the ranks . . . there would not be half the cheering and huzzaing that there is when General Jupiter Stonewall Jackson rides along our ranks."

Hill, not surprisingly, had a different view and in mid-November would describe Jackson as a "crazy old Presbyterian fool." "The Almighty will get tired," he predicted, "helping Jackson after a while, and then he'll get the d—ndest thrashing—and the shoe pinches, for I should get my share and probably all the blame, for the people will never blame Stonewall for any disaster."

A British officer who visited Jackson in October was significantly more impressed with the general and the devotion he inspired in his men. "He looks the hero that he is," he declared in an article published the following year, "[H]is thin compressed lips and calm glance, which meets you unflinchingly, give evidence of that firmness and decision of character for which he is so famous. . . . With such a leader men would go anywhere, and face any amount of difficulties; and for myself, I believe that, inspired by the presence of such a man, I should be perfectly insensible to fatigue, and reckon upon success as a moral certainty. . . . Jackson, like Napoleon, is idolized with that intense fervor which consisting of mingled personal attachment and devoted loyalty, causes them to meet death for his sake."

During the stay at Bunker Hill, Jackson's appearance received a decided upgrade when Jeb Stuart gave him a brand new uniform coat. Jackson had developed an exceedingly warm relationship with Stuart, whom he described to D. H. Hill as "my ideal of a cavalry leader; prompt, vigilant, and fearless." Hill would later recall seeing Stuart and Jackson sharing a hearty laugh when the former presented Jackson with a picture he had picked up during a raid into Pennsylvania that had the heading "Where is Stonewall Jackson?" Indeed, the coat Stuart presented Jackson was so fine that the shock of seeing the usually roughly attired Jackson dressed so handsomely led his African American servant Jim Lewis to almost drop a plate when he first saw him in it.

In addition to the upgrade in Jackson's appearance, the weeks after Antietam also saw Lee take advantage of recent legislation passed by the Confederate Congress to formally organize his army into two corps. He immediately recommended Longstreet and Jackson for corps command and promotion to the newly authorized rank of lieutenant general. "My opinion of the merits of General Jackson has been greatly enhanced," Lee informed Richmond, "He is true, honest, and brave; has a single eye to the good of the service and spares no exertion to accomplish his object."

Jackson's Second Corps, Army of Northern Virginia, was initially organized to consist of four divisions commanded respectively by Maj. Gen. Daniel H. Hill, Maj. Gen. Ambrose P. Hill, Brig. Gen. Jubal A. Early, and Brig. Gen. William B. Taliaferro. In all, the corps was composed of around 32,000 men and 23 batteries of artillery. To its commander's immense delight, the autumn of 1862 also saw a religious revival in Lee's army that Jackson did all he could to encourage. "It pleased our ever Merciful Father to visit my command with the rich outpouring of His Spirit," he delightedly informed a friend. "There was probably more than 100 inquiring the way of life in my old brigade. It appears to me that we may look for growing piety and many conversions in the army, for it is the subject of prayer."

Meanwhile, Jackson's desire for active operations was satisfied by a raid on Martinsburg in mid-October. While overseeing his men as they demolished all they could of the Baltimore and Ohio Railroad facilities in that town, a young woman carried her 18-month-old son toward Jackson and asked him to bless the child. In response, one observer later wrote, "the warrior-saint of another era, with the child in his arms, head bowed until his graying beard touched the fresh young hair of the child, pressed close to the shabby coat . . . closed his eyes, and seemed to be . . . occupied for a minute or two with prayer, during which we took off our hats and the young mother leaned her head over the horse's shoulder as if uniting in prayer." When Jackson was done, the mother thanked him and tearfully watched as he departed.

Finally, during the last week of October, the Federals began crossing the Potomac River east of the Blue Ridge. Lee responded by ordering Longstreet's command to move immediately to Culpeper Court House to block McClellan's attempt to reach a position on the Orange and Alexandria Railroad from which his army might cut the Army of Northern Virginia off from Richmond. Accompanying Longstreet personally, Lee also instructed Jackson to remain in the lower Shenandoah Valley to menace the Blue Ridge passes that led to the Federal flank and rear in the Loudoun Valley. From his headquarters at Winchester, Jackson immediately ordered his corps to move east to the Blue Ridge. There they would spend three weeks monitoring the Blue Ridge passes, during which Jackson acceded to a request from the daughter of one of his staff officers to sit for a photographer.

Fortunately for the Confederacy, Longstreet's command managed to reach Culpeper before the Federals, which contributed to Washington's decision during the first week of November to replace McClellan with Maj. Gen. Ambrose Burnside as commander of the Army of the Potomac. Burnside almost immediately decided to march his army to Falmouth, the small village just across the Rappahannock River from Fredericksburg. Once there, he intended to cross the Rappahannock River and take possession of the heights south of Fredericksburg before the Confederates could do so.

Fortunately for the Confederates, bungling in Washington over the delivery to Burnside of pontoon bridges to facilitate his crossing of the Rappahannock negated the advantages Burnside gained by the speed of his march to Falmouth. Thus, Lee was able to push Longstreet's command to Fredericksburg and claim possession of the heights outside the town before the Federals. Burnside's forces, though, far outnumbered Longstreet's small command. If he was to hold this line, Lee knew he needed Jackson's command.

On November 22, Jackson had anticipated this by putting his command on the march through a snowy Winchester. His men then pushed south to New Market before turning east to cross Massanutten Mountain. On November 24, Jackson's men crossed the Blue Ridge at Thornton's Gap and entered the Virginia Piedmont.

Shortly after reaching the Orange and Alexandria Railroad and putting his men into camp after a tough series of marches through cold, sleet, and snow, on November 28 Jackson received a note from his sister reporting he was now the father of a daughter. He promptly wrote back to inform his wife that he wished for the little girl to be named Julia, which Anna agreed to. "My mother," he explained, "was mindful of me when I was a helpless, fatherless child, and I wish to commemorate her." Although he had earlier expressed a preference for a son, explaining to his wife that "men had a larger sphere of usefulness than women," he nonetheless was ecstatic at the news and quickly reversed his earlier sentiments regarding the child's gender.

With his heart bursting with delight, the following morning Jackson put his men on the march toward Fredericksburg. Riding well ahead of them, he covered about 40 miles that day, following the roads that connected Orange Court House with Fredericksburg and managing to reach Lee's headquarters after night had fallen. By December 1, Jackson's men had all reached Fredericksburg and learned Lee had decided the Second Corps would form to the right of Longstreet's command and extend the Confederate line south and eastward along the right bank of the Rappahannock. To deal with the danger of a Federal attempt to turn the Confederate right by crossing the Rappahannock downstream from Fredericksburg, Jackson found himself compelled to extend his line some 20 miles by sending D. H. Hill's division to Port Royal.

HOW HORRIBLE IS WAR

On December 11, Burnside ended the uncertainty as to his intention that had necessitated the dispersal of Jackson's command by opening a bombardment on Fredericksburg and ordering an effort to establish a series of bridgeheads across the Rappahannock at and just below the town. Although Confederates posted in Fredericksburg put up a fierce fight, they were unable to prevent the Federals from crossing the river and seizing possession of the town. Lee responded by ordering a contraction of his line. Jackson's command on the right, he decided, would hold a line about two miles long along the heights south and west of Fredericksburg. At around 8:00 A.M., on December 12, A. P. Hill's division reached Hamilton's Crossing on the Richmond, Fredericksburg, and Potomac Railroad and began taking over the section of the line between that point and Longstreet's right whose main feature was an elevation known as Prospect Hill. Jackson then ordered Taliaferro's division to take up a position behind Hill's. He also directed Early and D. H. Hill to remain downriver, but to be prepared to move to Fredericksburg the instant orders arrived to do so.

As the Federals built up their forces in and around Fredericksburg on December 12, Lee and Stuart went over to Jackson's position to discuss the situation. They then rode forward to look over the enemy's dispositions and quickly concluded that it was pointless to keep Early's and D. H. Hill's commands so far down river. Jackson directed Early and Hill to immediately march their commands toward Fredericksburg. He then spent the rest of the day looking over his line, paying particular attention to how the artillery was posted.

A heavy fog greeted Jackson when he awoke the next morning. Both Early's and D. H. Hill's commands had arrived during the night and taken up their assigned positions in line after rough marches of 15 and 20 miles over roads covered in cold mud. Jackson put on his new uniform and began riding along the lines en route to a meeting at Lee's headquarters. The handsomeness of Jackson's attire aroused considerable curiosity among his men. "Ah, General," one man exclaimed when Jackson passed his section of the line, "you need not try to hide yourself in those clothes; we all know you too well for that." Another later recalled, "he looked so unlike our 'Old Jack' that very few noticed him, and none recognized him until he had passed. Then the old accustomed cheer to him went up with unusual vigor!"

Jackson's appearance also excited commentary at army headquarters, but this was quickly subsumed to the high command's concerns about the tactical situation. Jackson almost immediately proposed taking advantage of the heavy fog that blanketed the region to launch an attack on the Federals. Although Stuart endorsed the suggestion, Lee rejected it. He thought it better to allow the Federals to attack first, then follow up a successful repulse with a counterattack. As Jackson prepared to depart, Longstreet good-naturedly asked, "Jackson, what are you going to do with all those people over there?" Jackson replied sternly, "Sir, we will give them the bayonet." Jackson's zeal to engage the enemy was also evident to his men when he returned to them after the meeting at headquarters. "The troops cheered him wildly," one later wrote, "He gave us a sharp, searching, but not unkindly look, raised his cap, and rode rapidly on. His eyes seemed to be on fire, so eager was he for the fray."

By this time, the Union artillery had begun firing in preparation for an assault on the Confederate lines. Burnside planned for an attack on Jackson's position by one wing of his army, hoping it would break the Confederate line there, or at least induce the Confederates to weaken Longstreet's position sufficiently to allow the wing of the Federal army attacking it to achieve success.

As the fog began to lift at mid-morning, the Confederates got their first good glimpse at the strong Federal force confronting them. Shortly thereafter, the enemy moved against Jackson's position. Burnside gave Maj. Gen. William B. Franklin's command the task of attacking the Confederate right, but Franklin's efforts were initially frustrated by two pieces of artillery that Maj. John Pelham, the outstanding young commander of Stuart's horse artillery, managed to position on his flank. About an hour after Union artillery fire finally compelled Pelham to withdraw, the Federal infantry rushed forward, their advance inadvertently aiming for a section of swampy bottom land where a gap of several hundred yards existed in the section of A. P. Hill's line between Brig. Gen. James Lane's and Brig. Gen. James Archer's brigades.

As the Federals advanced, Jackson directed his artillery to wait for his signal before opening fire. Then, when the enemy's lines were less than a thousand yards away, Jackson gave it. The Federal line staggered but quickly regained its forward momentum and drove forward. At around 1:00 P.M., the Federal division commanded by Maj. Gen. George Meade (the very same officer for whom the fort where Jackson served as a young lieutenant in Florida was named) reached the swampy lowland and poured into the gap in Hill's line. They then surprised and overwhelmed a brigade commanded by Brig. Gen. Maxcy Gregg. Within minutes, a staff officer had reached Jackson's headquarters with the news. "General!" he reported, "The enemy have broken through. . . . General Gregg says he must have help or he and General Archer will both lose their position."

Jackson did not panic, for he knew he had plenty of manpower available to deal with Meade's command. The most important proved to be the men of Early's division, whose commander had been given orders to take up another section of the line from Jackson, but who decided to disobey those orders to instead go to Hill's assistance. Assisted by three brigades of Hill's command still in the fight, and the fact that the Federals failed to fully support Meade's efforts, Early was able to launch a powerful counterattack that drove Meade's men back. As Jackson watched his men restore their line, one man "saw him raise his hand & the expression on his face & the gesture so impressed me that I rode on behind him saying to myself, 'I will get the benefit of that prayer.'" Jackson then directed his guns to fire on the retreating Federals. Even though this provoked what proved to be an uneven artillery duel with the Federals, it was clear that Jackson's men had successfully thwarted the enemy's designs on their part of the field.

As the focus of Union efforts shifted to Longstreet's strongly positioned line, where they made a series of assaults that were exercises in futility with few parallels in American military history, Jackson decided during the late afternoon that the time had come to launch a counterattack. He sent orders to D. H. Hill and Taliaferro to lead the assault, with A. P. Hill's and Early's commands in support. However, those orders did not reach his subordinates in time for an attack to be made before sundown. Moreover, when Jackson ordered his artillery to open fire as a preliminary to the infantry's advance, he later wrote, "the enemy's artillery reopened, & so completely swept our front, as to satisfy me that the proposed movement should be abandoned."

To Jackson's intense frustration, the battle ended that evening with the Federals defeated, but the Confederate army unable to find an opportunity to follow up its defensive success. At a council of war that night, Jackson was the only one arguing for an attack. "Drive them into the river!" he cried out, "Drive them into the river!" The Federal army, however, backed by its powerful artillery, was simply too strong for there to be much prospect for success from a counterattack. Recognizing this, Lee sent his subordinates back to their commands with directions only to focus on improving their defensive positions in case the Federals renewed their attacks.

Jackson loyally complied with Lee's instructions. He also took the time during the early morning of December 14 to visit General Gregg, who had been mortally wounded in the battle. "Turn your thoughts to God," he advised the dying officer, "and to the world to which you go." After leaving to return to his headquarters, Jackson remarked to his staff, "How horrible is war!" "Horrible, yes," one man remarked, "but we have been invaded. What can we do?" Jackson sternly replied, "Kill them, sir! Kill every man!"

After a day marked by random exchanges of artillery and small arms fire, as well as an afternoon truce to collect the wounded and bury the fallen, Burnside began pulling his command back across the Rappahannock River on December 15. Frustrated that he had not been able to deliver a blow, Jackson remarked upon learning of the Federal retreat, "I am sorry that they are gone."

THE LAST WINTER

Jackson initially thought that he and his corps might return to the Shenandoah Valley for the winter of 1862–63. However, the fact that Burnside's massive army remained just across the Rappahannock River meant there was no way Lee would do anything to diminish the strength of the Army of Northern Virginia at Fredericksburg. Nonetheless, the Federals appeared sufficiently chastened by the outcome of the Battle of Fredericksburg to suggest active operations were over for the year and the time had come to go into winter quarters. (The Federals would attempt another offensive in late January, but bad weather prevented what became known as the "Mud March" from accomplishing any-thing other than to exacerbate discontent in the Army of the Poto-mac with Burnside, which contributed to Lincoln's decision to remove him from command on January 25.)

In the days following Fredericksburg, the Corbin family extended welcome hospitality to Jackson and his staff from their home, called Moss Neck Manor, located a little over 10 miles downstream from Fredericksburg. This led Jackson to decide he would make his head-quarters at Moss Neck for what would turn out to be a bitterly cold and unpleasant winter in terms of the weather.

The second photograph of Jackson made during the war, this was taken during his wife's visit to headquarters shortly before the opening of the Chan-cellorsville Campaign in April 1863. Despite the fact that she believed at that time "he never presented a finer appearance in health and dress" and took considerable care in arranging his appearance for the camera, Mrs. Jackson later lamented the photo captured "a sternness to his countenance that was not natural." (National Archives)

Jackson's mind also quickly turned to the prospects the end of active operations held for his personal situation. "I do hope," he wrote his wife, "that you and baby can come to see me before spring, as you can come on the railroad. Wherever I go, God gives me kind friends. . . . He continually showers blessings upon me; and that *you* should have been spared, and our darling little daughter given us, fills my heart with overflowing gratitude." He was especially delighted on Christmas, when he wrote to Anna, "Yesterday I received the baby's letter with its precious lock of hair. How I do want to see that precious baby!"

Still, Jackson would not consider going to North Carolina to see his wife and child. "[I]t is better for me," he informed Anna, "to remain with my command so long as the war continues. . . . If all our troops, officers & men were at their posts, we might through God's blessing, expect a more speedy termination of the war. . . . [W]hilst it would be a great comfort to see you, & my darling little daughter . . . duty appears to require me to remain with my command. It is important that these Hd. Qrs. set an example by remaining at the post of duty."

Nonetheless, Christmas 1862 was a very pleasant experience for Jackson. Local citizens, delighted to play host to one of the Confederacy's great heroes, supplied Moss Neck with a veritable bounty for the holiday. Thus, Jackson invited Lee, Stuart, and a number of other officers to have Christmas dinner with him at Moss Neck, where they feasted on turkey, biscuits, vegetables, ham, oysters, and wine. Stuart good-naturedly needled Jackson throughout the evening, and Lee even dropped his habitual reserve to join in on the fun.

That Lee could do so was testimony to the strong relationship he and Jackson had forged by the end of 1862. It was also evident in a letter Jackson wrote to a congressman on December 31 suggesting that the Shenandoah Valley be organized as an independent military department. "You must not think," he declared, "that I desire to be sent to the Valley, even if it should be made a Department. I would rather remain in a subordinate position . . . provided that my command is kept near my Commanding General." A few months later, Stuart confided to one of Jackson's associates that in August, "Gen. Lee came to us at Gordonsville with rather a low estimate of Jackson's ability;—but now he often wishes that he had many Jacksons."

Meanwhile, as his men turned the forests around Moss Neck into a city of winter huts, Jackson supervised the preparation of reports on the operations of his various commands in 1862. He also struggled to improve the lot of his men, who suffered from shortages of just about everything from wood and food to clothing to blankets and tents. All the time, he also did all he could to keep the men occupied and under strict discipline, in part by being decidedly stingy in the granting of officer furloughs.

Meanwhile, A. P. Hill continued to pursue his feud with Jackson despite Lee's best efforts to put off Hill's demands for a court martial to officially settle the matter. Jackson was also compelled to say farewell to brother-in-law D. H. Hill, whose irascible personality had finally driven Lee to the conclusion that he had worn out his welcome in the Army of Northern Virginia and led to his reassignment to duty in North Carolina. During what would be their last conversation, Jackson expressed concern about the degree to which people inside and outside the army had placed their hopes for success in him and other generals. "The manner in which the press, the army, and the people seem to lean upon certain persons is positively frightful," he confided, "They are forgetting God in the instruments he has chosen. It fills me with alarm."

Still, all was not gloom for Jackson during the winter months of 1862–63, which saw him turn 39 in January. His daughter and wife were doing well, with the former successfully fighting off a series of illnesses. In addition, a bright light entered Jackson's world in the form of young Jane Corbin, the six-year-old daughter of the proprietor of Moss Neck. A "sweet little child of six years," was how one member of the general's staff described her, "as happy and sunny a child as I ever saw. . . . She was the General's delight." She accompanied the general almost constantly as he went about his work, with the general regularly dropping the serious business of war to play with her, exhibiting a degree of joy and lightness that not only surprised, but astonished observers who thought they knew Jackson well. One afternoon, he noticed her hair was in her eyes and playfully asked what she had done with her comb. When she explained that she had lost it, Jackson promptly removed the gold braid from his cap with a knife and lovingly used it to tie her hair. He then placed his hands on her cheeks and remarked, "Janie, it suits a little girl like you better than it does an old soldier like me."

Jackson also continued his efforts to elevate the religious tone of his command. Of particular concern, given his desire to lead what he called a "converted army," was his command's deficiency in chaplains. When Reverend B. Tucker Lacy, one of Virginia's leading clergymen, arrived at Jackson's headquarters early in 1863 to offer his services as a regimental chaplain, Jackson extended an enthusiastic welcome. Jackson told Lacy that his main source of anxiety for the Confederate cause was not the Yankee army, but "the sin of the army and people." Jackson then invited Lacy to serve as chaplain for his entire corps. After a few weeks mulling over the offer, Lacy agreed to accept the post.

Jackson immediately donated $200 personally to support Lacy's efforts, as well as a horse. Jackson also made a point of regularly attending services held in a chapel the Stonewall Brigade had constructed, during which one man later recalled the general would "come quietly in among the soldiers and occupy a camp stool or modest seat and listen reverently to the singing and the sermons." With Jackson providing all the logistical and moral support Lacy could ask for, the religious character of the Second Corps saw a dramatic improvement over the winter that was a source of great satisfaction to its commander. "[T]hanks to an Ever Kind Providence," he declared, "I do not know where so many men brought together without any religious test exhibit such religious feeling."

As the harsh winter weather of February 1863 gave way to signs of spring in March, Jackson eagerly awaited the resumption of active operations—undoubtedly in no small part due to a desire for an alternative to the onerous task of writing reports that consumed much of his time during the winter. "We must make the coming campaign an exceedingly active one," he told Lacy. "Only thus can a weaker country cope with a stronger one. Our country must make up in activity what it lacks in strength. A defensive campaign can only be made successfully by taking the aggressive." What Jackson had in mind in this regard was suggested in February when cartographer Jedediah Hotchkiss received "secret orders from the General to prepare a map of the Valley of Va. extended to Harrisburg, Pa., and then on to Philadelphia."

Before operations could begin, though, tragedy struck. In mid-March, as Jackson began the process of closing up operations at Moss Neck and moving his headquarters in order to be closer to Lee's, Janie

Corbin contracted scarlet fever. It initially appeared that she was do-ing well and would recover, but this proved not to be the case. As Jackson was relocating his headquarters on March 17, a staff officer informed him that Janie had died. Jackson was heartbroken. Weeping with grief, he fell to his knees in prayer and directed his staff officer to return to Moss Neck and do all he could for the family. Shortly there-after, Jackson was again brought to tears on learning the Stonewall Brigade had assumed the task of burying Janie and her two cousins, who were also victims of the fever.

Two other factors during the late winter and early spring also un-doubtedly contributed to the zeal with which Jackson pursued his own spiritual development and promoted that of his men—as well as his eagerness to get on with the business of campaigning. The first was reports that his Unionist sister Laura in western Virginia was match-ing her sentiments with deeds, providing support and aid to Federal soldiers and surgeons—with some suggesting she was doing more than that. The other was his continuing separation from his wife and baby daughter. "I haven't seen my Wife for nearly a year & my home for nearly two years," he lamented in a letter to Anna, "I have never seen my sweet little Daughter." "Just to think," he wistfully declared in an-other message to her, "our baby is nearly three months old. Does she notice and laugh much? You have never told me how much she looks like her mother. I tell you, I want to know. . . . If you could hear me talking to my *esposa* in the mornings and evenings, it would make you laugh, I'm sure. It is funny the way I talk to her when she is hundreds of miles away."

Jackson's long separation from his wife finally ended in April. With no indication of significant activity on the part of the Federal army, now commanded by Maj. Gen. Joseph Hooker, Jackson wrote his wife to propose she and the child pay a visit. She eagerly agreed to do so. On April 17, Jackson learned Anna and Julia had arrived in Richmond and had been extended the use of the governor's mansion for their ac-commodations. Three days later, Jackson asked the governor to send Anna and the baby on to Guinea Station. Upon their arrival, his wife later recalled that though the day was rainy, "His face was all sunshine and gladness; and, after greeting his wife, it was a picture, indeed to see his look of perfect delight and admiration as his eyes fell upon that baby! . . . [A]s we drove in a carriage to Mr. Yerby's [the Thomas Yerby house was located a short ride from the J. P. Yerby farm where Jackson had his headquarters], his face reflected all the happiness and delight that were in his heart."

Upon Jackson's arrival at the Yerby house, the soldiers there raised a loud cheer. The Jacksons then entered the house where, his wife later wrote, the general "speedily divested himself of his overcoat, and, taking the baby in his arms, he caressed her with the tenderest affection, and held her long and lovingly." When she looked back on her visit, Anna proclaimed, "I never saw him look *so well*. He seemed to be in excellent health & looked handsomer than I had ever seen him . . . he was so full of happiness at having us with him & seeing & caressing his sweet babe, that I thought we had never been so blest & so happy in our lives." Others noted how happy Jackson was and how his delight in his child was evident in the constant attention he devoted to her. He held her as often as he could and even when she slept in her cradle, "would often kneel over her cradle, and gaze upon her little face with the most rapt admiration."

On April 23, Jackson held Julia as Chaplain Lacy baptized the child and officially christened her Julia Laura Jackson. Three days later, Jackson and his wife worshiped together for the first time in months, participating in an outdoor service in which General Lee was also among the thousand or so who attended. So delighted was Jackson with his family's company that he agreed during their nine-day visit to gratify his wife's request that he have his picture taken by a photographer from Richmond who had recently come up to visit the army. "After arranging his hair myself," she later wrote, "which was unusually long for him, and curled in large ringlets, he sat in the hall of the [Yerby] house." He wore the uniform coat that Stuart had given him, and despite the joy Anna's and Julia's presence had aroused in him, the photographer managed to capture an image of the general's face expressing what Anna later called "a sternness to his countenance that was not natural."

On April 29, though, the business of war returned. That day, an officer on Early's staff notified Jackson that the Federal army had crossed the river just below Fredericksburg. Jackson immediately informed his wife that it was time for her and the baby to return to Richmond. The task of escorting them was given to her brother Joseph and Reverend

Lacy. Jackson then mounted his horse and rode off to tend to military matters, but not before taking, in Anna's words, "an affectionate leave" from her and Julia.

Jackson rode over to Hamilton's Crossing and learned the Federals had in fact crossed the river at Deep Run and that Early had deployed his command with three regiments serving as pickets. Jackson then went over to army headquarters and found Lee trying to sort out what was going on in response to reports that seemed to be coming from nearly every point on the compass regarding Federal movements. Lee directed Jackson to reinforce Early, but to also be prepared to move elsewhere if events required it. As Jackson returned to his command with the prospect of active operations again before him, one man noticed, "his bearing became quicker, energetic, more lofty. The whole man energized and inspired."

Chapter 11

ALLOW NOTHING
TO STOP YOU

WITH MY WHOLE CORPS

"Fighting Joe" Hooker had conceived an inspired plan of operations. While part of his army distracted the Confederates at Fredericksburg, the bulk of it moved upriver to cross the Rappahannock and Rapidan Rivers in an attempt to outmaneuver the Confederate defenses at Fredericksburg. On top of this, he ordered his cavalry to conduct a massive raid against Lee's communications. These three elements of the plan, combined with the fact that all but two of Longstreet's divisions, plus Longstreet himself, were at that time more than one hundred miles away conducting operations south of the James River around Suffolk, would—Hooker believed—at least compel the Confederates to abandon their strong position behind the Rappahannock. If they did not, then they would be crushed by a Federal army that outnumbered Lee's by more than two to one.

Initially, the Federal plan worked magnificently. Although the cavalry raid would not accomplish much, Hooker was able to get three corps army across the Rappahannock and Rapidan Rivers before Lee could figure out what exactly was going on and they secured possession

of the crossroads at Chancellorsville on April 30. The evening before, Jackson had received a letter from Anna in which she expressed
hopes that "I may be permitted to come back to you again in a few
days. I am much disappointed in not seeing you again. But I commend
you . . . to the merciful Keeping of the God of battles & do pray most
earnestly for the success of our army. . . . Oh! that our Heavenly
Father may *preserve & guide & bless you*, is my most earnest prayer."

Jackson arose early on April 30 and rode over to headquarters to
discuss the situation with Lee. He learned Lee had received word from
Stuart about the Federal crossing of the rivers and ordered a division
commanded by Maj. Gen. Richard Anderson to move west toward
Chancellorsville. Lee then asked Jackson to ride with him, and the
two men proceeded to high ground from where they could survey the

William L. Sheppard's Lee and Jackson in Council on the Night of May 1,
which first appeared in Battles and Leaders of the Civil War, *offers a more
intimate and accurate portrayal than Everett B. D. Julio's grand portrait of the
great Confederate commanders as they planned their maneuvers at Chancellorsville.
(Johnson, Robert Underwood and Clarence Clough Buel, eds.,* Battles and
Leaders of the Civil War. *New York: The Century Co., 1887.)*

scene in Fredericksburg. As they did so, Jackson urged Lee to attack the Federals that had crossed the Rappahannock. Although he questioned the practicality of Jackson's proposal, Lee replied, "If you think it can be done, I will give the orders for it." Jackson then, perhaps sensing how reluctantly Lee had given his assent, told his commanding general that he thought it wise to first investigate the matter further. As rain fell through the afternoon, Jackson reluctantly came to the conclusion that his plan was not feasible and advised Lee upon returning to army headquarters that it would be "inexpedient to attack here."

By this point, Lee had concluded that the Federal force at Fredericksburg was merely a diversion designed to distract attention from Hooker's forces at Chancellorsville. He advised Jackson that he would be sending Maj. Gen. Lafayette McLaws's division—which along with Anderson's were the only two from Longstreet's command still with the army—west that night to assist Anderson. He then told Jackson he wanted him to take three of his divisions west the following morning "up to Anderson," and upon his arrival to "make arrangements to repulse the enemy." Jackson's fourth division, Early's, would remain at Fredericksburg to watch the Federals there.

When Jackson returned to his headquarters after his conference with Lee, he was informed that there was talk of the army retreating from its current position. "Who said that?" a manifestly irritated Jackson exclaimed, "No, sir, we have not a thought of retreat. We will attack them." Determined to reach Anderson and McLaws as soon as possible without subjecting his men to a night march, Jackson sent orders to A. P. Hill, Brig. Gen. Robert Rodes, and Brig. Gen. Raleigh Colston to have their divisions ready to leave Hamilton's Crossing at three the next morning. With Jackson at the head, and Rodes in the lead, followed by Hill and Colston, the Second Corps began their march on May 1 right on schedule. At around 8:30 A.M., Jackson found Anderson's command posted on high ground blocking the Orange Turnpike near Zoan Church. Anderson reported that his men and McLaws had been actively digging in anticipation of fighting a defensive battle.

Jackson immediately instructed Anderson to halt his defensive preparations and told him and McLaws to prepare to advance. He directed McLaws to push his division west toward Chancellorsville along the Orange Turnpike, while to the south Anderson's command would

Everett B. D. Julio's
The Last Meeting of
Lee and Jackson, *one
of the truly grand and
iconic works of
Confederate art.
(Library of Congress)*

move west following the Orange Plank Road. McLaws, Jackson hoped, could hold the Federals in front, while Anderson, supported by the entire Second Corps, reached a point from which they could assault the Federal right flank.

The previous evening, Hooker had issued a proclamation to his troops declaring "the operations of the last three days have determined that our enemy must ingloriously fly, or come out from his defenses and give us battle on our own ground, where certain destruction awaits him." However, the Federal commander's plan for May 1 did not consist of waiting passively for the enemy. Instead, he ordered his men to advance east out of the heavily wooded region around Chancellorsville known as the Wilderness toward open ground closer to Fredericksburg. Two divisions were to take the River Road, while a third, backed by an entire corps, advanced along the Orange Turnpike, and another corps followed the Orange Plank Road.

Thus, by midmorning both forces were moving toward a collision. It came a little after 11:00 A.M., when McLaws's advance made contact with the Federals on the turnpike. McLaws promptly reported this to Jackson and informed him that the enemy in his front appeared formidable. Jackson directed McLaws to halt his advance and sent over some artillery to support his division. Meanwhile, Jackson rode along the Orange Plank Road hoping to find the enemy flank. However, upon receiving evidence that a strong body of Federal infantry was moving toward him along the road, Jackson became concerned about his own flanks and slowed his advance. This concern proved unfounded, for shortly after making contact with the Confederates, Hooker ordered his columns to pull back into the Wilderness toward Chancellorsville.

At around 1:00 P.M., Lee arrived on the scene. With their men cheering them as they rode along the line, Lee and Jackson discussed the situation. Lee fully endorsed Jackson's actions to that point, but it quickly became evident they needed more information regarding Hooker's position and intentions. Thus, Lee decided to conduct a personal reconnaissance of the situation to the north and left direction of the situation along the Plank Road in Jackson's hands.

By 2:30 P.M., Jackson felt he had enough information to resume the advance and sent a message to McLaws stating he was "pressing on up the Plank Road . . . you will press on up the Turnpike, as the enemy is falling back." When the head of his column reached the Plank Road's intersection with a road that ran south and west toward an old iron furnace known as Catherine's Furnace, Jackson ordered a brigade commanded by Brig. Gen. Ambrose Wright to see if it could find the Union right flank.

By 5:30 P.M., Jackson himself had ridden to Catherine's Furnace, where he encountered Stuart, who undoubtedly informed him that the Federals were strongly posted about a mile to the north. The two generals conducted a brief reconnaissance, then posted some artillery and watched as it opened fire. The Federal artillery in the distance immediately fired back, and Jackson and Stuart found themselves in an exceedingly uncomfortable place. "General Jackson," Stuart exclaimed, "we must move from here." After seeing to the treatment of a mortally wounded member of Stuart's staff, Jackson made his way back to the Plank Road.

At around 7:00 P.M., Jackson reached the intersection of the Plank and Catherine's Furnace roads and found Lee there. Lee asked Jackson what he had seen at Catherine's Furnace. Jackson reported that Stuart and Wright had encountered stiff resistance that indicated a major effort there held little prospect of success. Nonetheless, the fact that the Federals had pulled back earlier in the day into the Wilderness suggested to Jackson that they had little stomach for a fight. "By tomorrow morning," he predicted, "there will not be any of them this side of the river."

Lee disagreed and, with only Early's division holding off the Federals at Fredericksburg, was anxious to figure out some way to attack Hooker successfully. The roughness of the terrain and strength of the Federal positions north of and along the Turnpike or Plank Roads, Lee had already determined, meant that there was little prospect of success for an attack against Hooker's left or center. It was unclear, though, whether the possibility of a successful attack against the Federal right existed until Stuart arrived and reported that one of his subordinates had found Hooker's right flank and determined it was in fact vulnerable.

Lee asked Stuart about the routes that might be taken to reach Hooker's flank. Stuart did not have an answer but promised to find out. After Stuart departed down the road to Catherine's Furnace on his reconnaissance, Lee and Jackson were left to wait. As they did so, two scouts arrived who confirmed Lee's sense that there was little to be gained attacking the Union left and center. Lee then asked aloud, "How can we get at those people?"

He and Jackson then intently studied a map of the area by the light of a candle. Jackson watched as Lee traced with his finger the roads that seemed to lead to the vulnerable portion of Hooker's line that Stuart had reported. The two men quickly agreed on the best—indeed really only—course of action available to them if they did not wish to fulfill Hooker's prediction that they would "ingloriously fly" or give the Federals "battle on our own ground, where certain destruction awaits." Jackson would take his three divisions and attempt to maneuver around the Federal army and reach a position from which it could attack from the west. Stuart's cavalry, it was quickly decided also, would screen the march. Beyond that, though, the details regarding the route to be taken were not clear. Nonetheless, Jackson assured Lee, "My troops will move at four o'clock." He then departed to get some rest.

After only about two hours of sleep, Jackson got up and sought the comfort of a campfire, next to which there was an abandoned Union cracker box where he could sit. Shortly thereafter, Reverend Lacy came up to him and accepted Jackson's offer of a seat on another cracker box. "The enemy are in great force in Chancellorsville," Jackson confided to Lacy, "To dislodge them by frontal attack would cost a fearful loss." He then asked Lacy, who had family in the area, "Do you know of any way by which we could flank either their right or left?"

"There is a blind road," Lacy replied, "leading from the furnace, nearly parallel to the Plank Road, which falls into a road running northward, which again would lead into the Plank Road three and a half to four miles above Chancellorsville." Jackson immediately pulled a map from his pocket and asked Lacy to, "Take this . . . and mark it down." After Lacy did so, Jackson noted with disappointment that the route Lacy traced out, "will go within the line of the enemy's pickets. Do you know no other?"

Lacy said he did not, for he had not personally followed the furnace road himself. But, he remarked, perhaps the Wellford family that operated Catherine's Furnace might know and be able to provide a guide. Jackson immediately awoke his mapmaker Jedediah Hotchkiss and told him and Lacy to go to the Wellford house. He directed Lacy to find out if the road network would support the movement and, "Send Hotchkiss back with the information. You get me a guide." After Hotchkiss and Lacy departed, Jackson sat back down in front of the fire, where he was shortly thereafter joined by A. L. Long of Lee's staff. Seeing Jackson shivering through the chilly night, Long got the general some coffee.

At around 3:30 A.M., Hotchkiss and Lacy returned to find Lee and Jackson seated on cracker boxes discussing the situation. Hotchkiss reported that they had learned from the Wellfords of a road that provided a relatively secure route around the Federal army that could support artillery as well as infantry. Jackson eagerly listened as Hotchkiss described how the roughly 12-mile route ran south from Catherine's Furnace, then traveled west to its intersection with a north–south byway known as the Brock Road. Upon reaching the Brock Road, the column would turn south and after a few hundred yards turn right onto a road that paralleled the Brock Road for a few miles, but that was better concealed from the Federals than the Brock Road was. After moving north until the side road rejoined Brock Road, a marching column would take the Brock Road to its intersection with the Orange Plank Road. Reaching the Plank Road would place the Confederates about two miles beyond the area around Wilderness Church where Hooker's western flank was reported to be.

When Hotchkiss was done, Lee turned to the commander of the Second Corps and said, "General Jackson, what do you propose to do?" Jackson traced Hotchkiss's route on a map and replied, "Go around here." "What do you propose," Lee asked, "to make the movement with?" "With my whole corps," Jackson replied. Lee then asked, "What will you leave me?" "The divisions of Anderson and McLaws," Jackson said. After a brief pause in which Lee contemplated what exactly they were getting ready to do, the army commander turned to Jackson and said, "Well, go on."

As Jackson eagerly anticipated the task of implementing the plan, Hotchkiss later recalled he had "an eager smile upon his face." Jackson and Lee continued discussing the details of the plan until about 5:00 A.M., when Lee closed their conversation by assuring Jackson that "General Stuart will cover your movements with his cavalry." As he began to leave, Jackson saluted Lee and remarked, "My troops will move at once, sir!"

Not until 7:30 A.M., though, was Jackson able to get the lead elements of his command on the march. With Charles Wellford, the son of the proprietor of Catherine's Furnace, and another man as their guides, Stuart's cavalry led the march, followed by Rodes's division. Colston's division was next, while Hill's brought up the rear.

As his men began trudging down the road to Catherine's Furnace, Jackson was riding Little Sorrel forward to reach the head of the column when he saw General Lee standing by the road. He pulled up to talk with his commanding officer. What exactly they said to each other during this brief encounter is lost to history. But witnesses to the scene later recalled being impressed with how animated and eager Jackson was to execute the plan the two had agreed on. At one point Jackson gestured emphatically to the west, with Lee nodding assent to whatever point Jackson was trying to impress on his commander. Shortly thereafter, Jackson departed down the road to Catherine's Furnace. Lee and Jackson would never see each other again.

Jackson's twin concerns as he joined his men on the march were that their movements be made quickly and that they go undetected. His hopes in regard to the former were largely realized. The head of the 10-mile long column of about 30,000 men, who marched four abreast along the narrow roads that led to their destination, reached the Orange Plank Road successfully early in the afternoon.

Spirits were high among Jackson's men even though, as one man later recalled, "The day was very warm, the route poor. . . . We did not know and did not care where we were going." Jackson rode up and down his marching columns throughout the morning, urging his men to "press forward, press forward" and "see that the column is closed." "Never can I forget the eagerness and intensity of Jackson on that march," a member of Jackson's staff later recalled, "His face was pale, his eyes flashing. . . . Every man in the ranks knew that we were engaged in some great flank movements, and they eagerly responded and pressed on at a rapid gait." As a unit of North Carolinians moved through the afternoon, one of its members later recalled seeing a courier come "riding from the rear, saying General Jackson is coming, but no cheering. We stepped to the side of the road again and along came Gen. Jackson on his long, gaunt sorrel horse in a long gallop with his hat raised but not a word spoken."

Jackson reached the Brock Road's intersection with the Orange Plank Road at about 2:00 P.M. There he encountered cavalry officer Brig. Gen. Fitzhugh Lee and was told, "General, if you will ride with me, halting your columns here, out of sight, I will show you the enemy's right." Jackson did so and rode forward with Lee to a cleared rise on the Burton farm from where they had a clear view of much of the Federal line. That the Federals were unprepared to deal with anything the magnitude of what Jackson was planning was evident. Their arms were stacked, and the bluecoated soldiers of Maj. Gen. Oliver O. Howard's XI Corps were lazing around camp fires playing cards, talking, and relaxing with it seemed not a care in the world. "I watched him closely as he gazed upon Howard's troops," Lee recalled after the war,

His eyes burned with a brilliant glow, lighting up a sad face. His expression was one of intense interest, his face was colored slightly with the paint of approaching battle, and radiant at the success of his flank movement. . . . To the remarks made to him while the unconscious line of blue was pointed out, he did not reply once during the five minutes he was on the hill, and yet his lips were moving. From what I have read and heard of Jackson since that day, I know now what he was doing then. Oh! "beware of rashness" General Hooker. Stonewall Jackson is praying in full view and in rear of your right flank!

However, the fact that the Federal front was facing the Orange Plank Road troubled Jackson, as he wanted to hit their flank. Thus, he agreed with Lee that the best course of action would be to order his men to resume their march north along the Brock Road until they reached the Orange Turnpike. "Tell General Rodes," he instructed Lee, "to move across the Old plank-road; halt when he gets to the Old Turnpike, and I will join him there." "Near 3 p.m.," Jackson scribbled a short note to General Lee at army headquarters reporting, "The enemy has made a stand at Chancellor's [Dowdall's Tavern], which is about 2 miles from Chancellorsville. I hope as soon as practicable to attack. I trust that an ever kind Providence will bless us with great success. . . . The lead division is up & the next two appear to be well closed."

Jackson would not have all three of his divisions available for the attack, though, for his hope that his march would go undetected was not completely fulfilled. During the morning, Federal soldiers under the command of Maj. Gen. Daniel Sickles spotted Jackson's column as it turned south at Catherine's Furnace. Sickles reported this to Hooker, who made a personal investigation of the report and also caught sight of Confederates moving south. Finally, at around noon, Hooker authorized Sickles to advance and harass the enemy column. Sickles did and managed to overrun the Georgia regiment at the rear of Jackson's column during the afternoon. This compelled Hill to turn around two brigades from his division. They succeeded in containing the Federal advance but in the process ensured that Hill's entire command would not be able to keep pace with Jackson's other two divisions as they moved to the Orange Turnpike, nor could they participate in the afternoon's attack.

The action also had the effect, though, of enhancing Jackson's prospects for success against Howard, for Sickles's advance had left

Howard's corps isolated. Nonetheless, even this need not have been fatal for the Federals had Howard acted on a warning from Hooker during the morning that "we have good reason to suppose the enemy is moving to our right. Please advance your pickets for purposes of observation as far as may be safe in order to obtain timely information of their approach." Nor would the Confederate opportunity have been so great had orders to Federal corps commander Maj. Gen. John Reynolds to march his command to a position from where they could assist Howard not miscarried.

To the great good fortune of the Confederacy, though, Howard and the commander of the first of the divisions that would face Jackson had not taken seriously the prospect of an attack on their position, and Reynolds would not arrive until it was too late. Thus, Jackson found a magnificent tactical opportunity before him as he deployed Rodes's and Colston's divisions in mile-and-a-half-long battle lines astride the Orange Turnpike about a mile east of its intersection with the Brock Road. As his command moved into position, Jackson noted that both division commanders, as well as many of their subordinates, shared his connection with VMI and declared, "The Institute will be heard from today."

Shortly after reaching the turnpike, Jackson dismissed and expressed his appreciation to Jack Hayden, who along with Wellford had so ably guided the column. Before departing, Hayden turned to Jackson and said, "I desire you to do me one favor." "What is it, sir?" the general asked. "Take care of yourself," remarked Hayden.

Jackson directed Rodes to make the high ground on which the Talley farm was located the objective of the lead division's advance and to press on from there as far as Dowdall's Tavern. Colston would support and take over the battle when Rodes's advance stalled, which Jackson anticipated happening around Dowdall's, then continue pressing forward. "Under no circumstances," he repeatedly admonished his subordinates as they prepared to advance, "was there to be any pause in the advance."

Finally, at around 5:15 p.m., all was ready. Jackson turned to the commander of his lead division. "Are you ready, General Rodes?" "Yes, sir!" an enthusiastic Rodes declared. Jackson replied, "You can go forward then."

For the Federals, one Confederate officer later recalled, "The surprise was complete. A bolt from the sky would not have startled half as much . . . a solid wall of gray, forcing their way through the timber and bearing down upon them like an irresistible avalanche." Only two Union regiments were facing westward when Jackson's battle line suddenly appeared in front of them. They were quickly shattered. Rodes's men then pushed forward to overwhelm a hastily organized Federal defensive line around Wilderness Church. They then broke a final, valiant attempt by elements from the Eleventh Corps to put up resistance. "Press on! Press on!" Jackson shouted to his men as they advanced. By 7:15 P.M., though, fading daylight and increasing confusion in the Confederate lines, an unavoidable consequence of the effort it had taken to overrun three enemy lines and the fact that much of Jackson's command made its advance through thick woods, combined to begin arresting the momentum of the attack. "We could hardly tell which Reg. or Brig. we were in," one man later recalled, "that however made no difference, as we never stopped to learn who did this or that, but our watchward was onward."

As his men continued pushing east toward the point where the turnpike intersected a road that linked it with U.S. Ford on the Rappahannock, Jackson urged his men forward. If that road could be secured, Hooker's line of retreat might be cut off. Rodes, though, was already immensely pleased at what his command had accomplished and urged Jackson to "give them a big name in your report." "I shall take great pleasure in doing so," Jackson replied, "and congratulate you and your command." At the same time, though, Rodes and Colston endeavored to impress on Jackson the fact that after having made a tough march and experiencing two hours of heavy fighting, their commands were in no condition to continue the advance through the darkness. Jackson finally agreed to halt their advance and sent orders to Hill to push his command forward to resume the advance.

WOUNDING

While he waited for Hill, Jackson decided to ride forward. One of his staff officers, seeing him out in front of the skirmish line, remarked, "General, don't you think this is the wrong place for you?" "The danger is over!" Jackson replied, "The enemy is routed. Go back and tell A. P. Hill to press right on." Shortly thereafter, Jackson ran into Brig. Gen. James Lane, commander of the brigade of North Carolinians who were posted astride the Orange Plank Road in advance of the rest of the Confederate army. "My Carolinians are in line," Lane reported, "I am looking for General Hill to ascertain if I should begin the advance." Jackson responded, "Push right ahead, Lane."

Hill rode up shortly thereafter and learned Jackson wanted Lane's brigade to advance along the Plank Road toward Chancellorsville while the rest of his division pushed north toward U.S. Ford. "How long before you will be ready to advance," Jackson asked. "In a few minutes," Hill replied, "as soon as I can finish relieving General Rodes." "Do you know the road from Chancellorsville to the United States Ford?" Jackson asked. When Hill replied, "I have not travelled over it for many years," Jackson ordered an engineer officer, J. Keith Boswell, to accompany Hill. "[W]hen you reach Chancellorsville," Jackson directed, "allow nothing to stop you! Press on to the United States Ford!"

Jackson then decided to conduct a personal reconnaissance to see what was in front. Riding Little Sorrel, accompanied by a few staff

Jackson reels in the saddle after his wounding late on May 2, 1863, in Kurz and Allison's 1889 lithograph Battle of Chancellorsville. (*Library of Congress*)

officers, and followed by Hill and his staff (including Boswell, who had rather ominously noted in a letter home the previous month that "Strange as it may seem, not one of Genl. Jackson's staff has ever been killed. . . . I suppose his prayers have shielded us"), Jackson pushed east along the Mountain Road, a small path that paralleled the Plank Road. Upon reaching a point between Lane's main line and skirmish line, Jackson spent a few minutes listening to the sounds coming from the Federal lines a few hundred yards away. He then decided to return to his own lines and began retracing his steps along the Mountain Road. Shortly thereafter he turned Little Sorrel to the left to reach the Plank Road, about 60 yards from the section of Lane's line held by the 18th North Carolina.

As he did so, what had been the usual scattered gunfire that cut through the dark whenever two armies were in close contact with each other after a day of battle suddenly increased. One of Jackson's staff officers responded by shouting in the direction of the Confederate lines, "Cease firing! You are firing into your own men!" An officer in the 18th North Carolina, understandably alarmed that a party of mounted men were riding toward him from the direction of the Federal army, cried out, "Who gave that order? It's a lie! Pour it to them, boys!"

Jackson was struck three times. One bullet shattered his upper left arm just below the shoulder, while one blew a hole in his left forearm and another slammed into his right hand. Jackson reeled as a terrified Little Sorrel began dashing about and ran his master's face into the branch of an oak tree, which severely scratched Jackson's face. Two members of Jackson's entourage, Richard Wilbourn and William Wynn, helped him get Little Sorrel under control. "All my wounds," the severely dazed general remarked in amazement, "are by my own men." "I fear my arm is broken," he replied when asked whether he was hurt. Wilbourn asked him to try and move his fingers and when Jackson could not, asked, "General, what can I do for you?" Jackson inquired as to whether there was much blood. Wilbourn asked, "Where were you struck?" "About halfway between the elbow and shoulder," Jackson replied. "Is it very painful?" Wilbourn asked, "Are you hurt anywhere else?" After Jackson informed him of the injury to his right hand and finding heavy bleeding and evidence of broken bones upon reaching under the general's clothing, Wilbourn told Jackson, "I will have to cut off your sleeve before I can do anything for you." "Well," Jackson replied, "you had better take me down too."

Jackson was so weak that it took considerable effort for Wilbourn and Wynn to get him off Little Sorrel. They then carried the general to a small tree, with Wilbourn expressing amazement that anyone in their party was still alive. "Yes," Jackson quietly remarked, "It is providential." After setting Jackson down by a tree and dispatching Wynn to go find Hunter McGuire, Jackson's surgeon, with strict instructions not to let any of the troops he encountered find out what had happened, Wilbourn began working on Jackson. At this point, others began arriving on the scene, including A. P. Hill and Jackson's brother-in-law Joseph Morrison. "I have been trying to make the men cease firing," Hill informed Jackson, "I am sorry to see you wounded and hope you are not hurt much."

"My arm," Jackson replied," is broken . . . very painful." After learning Jackson was also wounded in the right hand, Hill removed Jackson's gloves as Wilbourn cut away Jackson's left sleeve. With Jackson's head resting on Hill's left leg, they then bandaged up Jackson's wounds, with Wilbourn tying a handkerchief around Jackson's upper left arm, a task interrupted briefly by the sudden appearance of two obviously lost Union soldiers only a few yards away. Before they could do any damage Hill directed two nearby couriers to seize them and they surrendered quietly. Shortly thereafter a surgeon attached to one of Hill's brigades arrived on the scene and offered a litter. After quickly examining Jackson, Surgeon Richard Barr departed to find his medical equipment. Upon locating a tourniquet, Barr returned but while examining the effect of Wilbourn's dressing decided to leave Jackson's left arm as it was.

Hill then departed to exercise the duties that came with command of the Second Corps, which had passed into his hands with Jackson's wounding. "I will keep your accident from the knowledge of the troops," he assured Jackson. "Thank you," Jackson replied. After Hill departed, Morrison, after a quick reconnaissance in which he saw Union artillery taking up a position that was uncomfortably close, decided Jackson needed to be moved. Jackson rose to his feet as the Federal gunners opened fire. As they proceeded west, Jackson's legs were uneasy as they passed by some of Hill's men, who despite efforts to conceal his identity quickly discerned who the injured man was.

Shortly thereafter a litter team Barr had called for was encountered and Jackson was carefully placed on a stretcher. As they carried the general, James Johnson, the Virginia private holding the left front of the litter, was struck by Union artillery fire. Jackson fell to the ground heavily as the other men carrying the stretcher lay down in an attempt to avoid Johnson's fate. As soon as they felt out of danger from the Union artillery, the group resumed carrying Jackson, but shortly thereafter one of the bearers tripped on a grape vine and the general once again came down hard on the ground. Jackson, with a torn artery added to his injuries at this point, was clearly in excruciating pain as he was lifted back onto the litter.

At that moment, brigade commander Brig. Gen. Dorsey Pender reached the group. "Oh, General," he remarked on seeing Jackson, "I hope you are not seriously wounded." Pender then warned Jackson that the Federal artillery fire had inflicted such damage that he thought he would "have to retire my troops to re-form them." Jackson immediately and sternly exclaimed, "You must hold your ground, General Pender; you must hold your ground, sir!"

After traveling another few hundred yards west, Jackson's party encountered Surgeon William Whitehead, who offered some whiskey to the injured Jackson and use of an ambulance. The wagon then traveled to Dowdall's Tavern, where Dr. McGuire finally located the group. McGuire found Jackson already out of the ambulance and placed on his litter next to the Orange Plank Road. "I hope you are not much hurt, General," McGuire said. "I am badly injured, Doctor. I fear I am dying," Jackson replied. "I am glad you have come. I think the wound in my shoulder is still bleeding."

McGuire called for whiskey and morphine and began examining Jackson. "I found his clothes saturated with blood," McGuire later recalled, "and blood still oozing from the wound. I put my finger upon the artery above the wound & held it . . . then I readjusted the handkerchief which had been applied as a tourniquet, but which had slipped a little. Without this been done, he would probably have died in ten minutes." After doing this and being amazed at Jackson's stoicism during an excruciatingly painful procedure, McGuire made sure Jackson received whiskey and morphine. He then oversaw Jackson's placement in an ambulance and accompanied the general, keeping his finger pressed above the tourniquet to contain the bleeding, to the Second Corps's field hospital. Also riding in the ambulance was an injured Col. Stapleton Crutchfield, who when told Jackson's wounds were serious, exclaimed, "Oh my God!"

Shortly before midnight the ambulance reached the Second Corps's field hospital at Wilderness Tavern on the Orange Turnpike, where a special tent had been set up for Jackson. At around 2:00 A.M., McGuire decided Jackson's condition had stabilized enough for a full examination of his injuries. Before giving the general chloroform, McGuire warned Jackson that his wounds might necessitate amputation and asked permission to do so. "Yes, certainly, Doctor McGuire," Jackson replied, "Do for me whatever you think right." As Jackson breathed in the chloroform and began to lose consciousness, he was heard saying, "What an infinite blessing . . . blessing . . . blessing."

It did not take long for McGuire to determine Jackson's left arm would have to be amputated. When Jackson awoke early on May 3, he found the bullet removed from his right hand, plaster applied to the wounds on his face, and his left arm gone. After drinking a little coffee, he fell back asleep. At around 4:00 A.M., staff officer Sandie Pendleton informed McGuire that he had to see Jackson to discuss the command situation in the Second Corps. Hill had been wounded the previous evening, and it had been decided that Stuart would assume command of the corps. McGuire reluctantly agreed, but when Pendleton informed Jackson that Stuart was seeking guidance as to what he should do, the general's mental fog was evident. "I don't know. I can't tell," he remarked, "Say to General Stuart that he must do what he thinks best."

Back at army headquarters, Robert E. Lee's distress at Jackson's wounding was evident. Upon learning from Wilbourn that Jackson's wounds were serious, he remarked, "any victory is dearly bought that deprives us of the services of General Jackson for even a short time." Wilbourn then attempted to describe the details of Jackson's wounds, but Lee cut him off. "Oh don't talk about it," Lee exclaimed, "Thank God, it is no worse."

As Jackson awoke on May 3, a note arrived from Lee stating, "I have received your note informing me that you were wounded. I cannot express my regret at the occurrence. Could I have directed events, I should have chosen for the good of the country to have been disabled in your stead. I congratulate you on the victory which is due to your skill and energy." "General Lee is very kind," Jackson informed the staff officer who read the message to him, "but he should give the praise to God."

That day, as Jackson rested, he received reports of the fighting that continued to rage around Chancellorsville and ended with the Federal army pulling back closer to the Rappahannock River, a preliminary move to its recrossing of the river and returning to its camps a few days later. Nonetheless, during the afternoon, Lee sent a message to Jackson suggesting he be relocated to Guinea Station on the Richmond, Fredericksburg, and Potomac Railroad so he would be further away from danger. Jackson was initially dubious about doing so. If the Federals were to somehow seize the area around Wilderness Tavern, he remarked, "I am not afraid of them. I have always been kind to their wounded, and I am sure they will be kind to me." Nonetheless, when McGuire said he had no objection to moving him, Jackson agreed to Lee's proposal.

On May 4, Jackson rode an ambulance accompanied by McGuire and Crutchfield 27 miles to Guinea Station. All along the ride, teamsters pulled to the side of the road and removed their hats in tribute upon being informed of who was in the ambulance. Local residents, McGuire later recalled, "At Spotsylvania and along the whole route . . . rushed to the ambulance, bringing all the food delicacies they had, and with tearful eyes blessed him & prayed for his recovery."

Along the way, Jackson chatted with McGuire. He expressed regret at the deaths of General Elisha Paxton, who had fallen on May 3 leading the Stonewall Brigade, and Keith Boswell (the same young officer who a few weeks earlier had expressed amazement at how no one from Jackson's staff had yet to be killed in action), and pride at the performance of his command. On explaining his plan on May 2 to interdict the Federal line of retreat to the Rappahannock, he expressed confidence that decisive results would have been achieved had this been done. "My men sometimes fail to drive the enemy from a position," he asserted. "They always fail to drive us away."

Finally, at around 8:00 P.M., Jackson's ambulance reached Fairfield, the home of Thomas Chandler and his wife, which was located just north of Guinea Station. Reverend Lacy had arranged with the

Chandlers to make available for Jackson's use the small, whitewashed frame structure that served as the family's office. When Jackson arrived, it was raining. He remarked to Thomas Chandler, "I am sorry I cannot shake hands with you, but one arm is gone and my right hand is wounded," and then he was taken to Chandler's office building. There, after having some bread and tea, Jackson went to sleep.

Chapter 12

UNDER THE SHADE OF THE TREES

THE LAST DAYS

Jackson awoke on May 5 in such good spirits and appearance that McGuire was impressed with his condition. During a conversation with a young member of his staff, Jackson even went so far as to proclaim his injuries a "blessing." When the officer replied by quoting a biblical verse, "All things work together for good to them that love God," Jackson exclaimed, "Yes! That's it! That's it!" Military matters were rarely far from his mind, though, and when word arrived that the Federals had managed to secure a defensive position that protected their line of retreat back across the Rappahannock, he lamented the prospect of no further advantage being gained by the Confederacy at Chancellorsville. "That is bad," he remarked, "very bad." That same day, Morrison traveled to Richmond—dodging Federal cavalry en route—to fill Mary Anna Jackson in on the details of her husband's injuries.

The following day, as his wife completed preparations for a trip north to Guinea Station, Jackson's condition took a turn for the worse. McGuire quickly became concerned that the general had developed pneumonia and immediately went to work applying every remedy he knew of for dealing with the illness. He also sent Reverend Lacy to Lee's headquarters to see if the army commander could spare the services of Dr. Samuel Morrison, who was then serving as chief surgeon on a division staff. As he departed Lee's tent, having succeeded in securing Morrison's services at Guinea Station, the commanding general asked him to give Jackson "my affectionate regards, and tell him to make haste and get well, and come back to me as soon as he can. He has lost his left arm but I have lost my right arm."

Anna Jackson arrived at Guinea Station at around noon that day, having brought the baby with her from Richmond. Though delighted to see her, Jackson was so weak that he was only able to remark, "I am glad to see you looking so bright" before falling back asleep. "He looked like a dying man," she later recalled, "the sight which there met my eyes was far more appalling, and sent such a thrill of agony and heart-sinking through me as I had never known before! Oh, the fearful change since last I had seen him! It required the strongest effort of which I was capable to maintain my self-control. . . . *Now* his fearful wounds, his mutilated arm, the scratches upon his face, and, above all, the desperate pneumonia, which was flushing his cheeks, oppressing his breathing, and benumbing his senses wrung my soul with such grief and anguish as it had never before experienced."

Reawakening to see his wife so distressed, Jackson lovingly admonished her. "My darling," he insisted, "you must cheer up and not wear a long face. I love cheerfulness and brightness in a sick-room." As Anna remained by her husband's side, leaving only from time to time to tend to baby Julia, he appreciatively declared, "My darling, you are very much loved . . . [and] one of the most precious little wives in the world."

When Lacy arrived, he and McGuire did all they could to help Jackson fight off his illness, giving him plenty of opiates to minimize his discomfort and help him sleep. At least three times that night, Jackson revealed where his mind had gone when asleep by shouting out military commands. "Order A. P. Hill to prepare for action," he commanded at one point, and at another he cried out, "Pass the infantry to the front."

When Jackson awoke the morning of May 8, he told his attendants that he was feeling better and was confident he would recover from his wounds and sickness. Breathing, however, clearly remained a chore for the general, and McGuire, Morrison, and two additional doctors whose services McGuire had acquired looked over the general. As they did, Jackson once again expressed his belief that his injuries "were given to me for some wise and good purpose." Still, he turned down Anna's offer to bring Julia into his room and, when she appealed to him to reconsider, assured her, "I do not believe I shall die at this time. I am persuaded the Almighty has yet a work for me to perform. . . . Do not be sad. I hope I may yet recover. Pray for me, but always in your prayers to use the petition, 'Thy will be done.'"

That Jackson's case was hopeless became clear the following day. Yet another doctor arrived from Richmond to see to the general and confirmed the sense of the others that his illness was fatal. At one point Jackson awoke to see his wife bathing him with tears running down her cheeks. "Anna," he remonstrated, "none of that, none of that." She then read to him from the Bible, which gave him great comfort. Shortly thereafter, she took on herself the task of telling her husband that death was imminent. "Let us ask Doctor McGuire," he replied, "what he says about it." When McGuire confirmed Anna's observation, Jackson remarked, "If it is the will of my Heavenly Father, I am perfectly satisfied."

During a visit by McGuire and some of the other doctors in the afternoon in which he remarked, "you think my condition dangerous, but I thank God, if it is his will, that I am ready to go. I am not afraid to die." Jackson asked to see Reverend Lacy. After pressing on Lacy the need for greater respect for the Sabbath in the Second Corps and listening to Lacy read from the Bible, Jackson declined the chaplain's offer to worship the next day and directed him to tend to the soldiers.

That night would be the last of Jackson's life. His wife and brother-in-law sang hymns to him as the doctors did all they could to alleviate his suffering. When McGuire and Morrison examined him early on May 10, they could see there was little time left. When they told Anna, she entered her husband's room and told him the doctors "say you must very soon be in Heaven. . . . Do you not feel willing to acquiesce in God's allotment, if He wills you to go today?" Jackson fought through his deep mental fog to twice reply, "I prefer it." Anna then tearfully told him, "before this day closes you will be with the blessed Saviour in His glory."

Later in the morning, after the doctors had checked on him, Anna returned. This time Jackson assured her, "Death is not so near. I may yet get well." At that point she broke down and, between her sobs, told her husband that was not going to happen. Jackson then called for McGuire and, upon his entering the room, remarked, "Doctor, Anna informs me that you have told her I am to die today. Is it so?" When McGuire confirmed this was the case, Jackson replied, "Very good, very good. It is all right."

Jackson and his wife then briefly and tenderly discussed the matter of where he was to be buried. When she suggested Lexington, he replied, "Yes, in Lexington, and in *my own plot*." Baby Julia was then brought into the room. "Little darling! Sweet one!" Jackson cried out with delight on seeing her, then caressed her head with his splintered right hand and said, "Little comforter, little comforter," before falling asleep.

When Jackson woke, staff officer Sandie Pendleton had entered the room. Pendleton informed him that, "The whole army is praying for you, General." "Thank God," Jackson replied, "They are very kind." He then remarked, "It is the Lord's day. My wish is fulfilled. I have always desired to die on a Sunday."

A few miles away nearly 2,000 soldiers had gathered for Reverend Lacy's service that Sunday. General Lee refused to accept Lacy's report that Jackson's case was hopeless. "Surely General Jackson must recover," Lee insisted, "God will not take him from us, now that we need him so much. Surely he will be spared to us, in answer to the many prayers which are offered for him." After the service, Lee told Lacy, "When you return, I trust you will find him better. When a suitable occasion offers, give him my love, and tell him that I wrestled in prayer for him last night as I never prayed, I believe, for myself."

Shortly thereafter, Jackson began slipping into a coma, the silence in the room punctuated by his shouting out, "Push up the columns! Hasten the columns!" "Pendleton," he cried out, "you take charge of that! Where's Pendleton? Tell him to push up the column!" Then, suddenly, he was quiet again. Shortly before 3:15 P.M., Jackson spoke his final words. These were words of peace, rather than war: "Let us cross over the river, and rest under the shade of the trees."

RETURN TO LEXINGTON

"It is a terrible loss," Lee wrote to his son Custis shortly after learning of Jackson's death. "I do not know how to replace him. Any victory would be dear at such a cost." Lee's response to news of Jackson's death was echoed throughout the Confederacy, with few places more affected than his hometown. "The rich perfumed spring air of Lexington," one man later remarked, "seemed darkened by the oppressive sorrow everywhere to be seen."

On Monday morning, May 11, Jackson's remains—minus the left arm, which after its amputation had been buried in the Lacy family cemetery near Wilderness Tavern—were placed on a train and began their last trip to Richmond. When they reached the capital late in the afternoon, a Confederate national flag was draped over the casket before it was taken to the governor's mansion along a road lined with weeping witnesses as, one observer wrote, "The sad tolling of the bells . . . and the dull thud of the minute guns alone broke the stillness." There Jackson's body, after being embalmed, rested in state. The

General Lee's last visit to Stonewall Jackson's grave, *painted by Louis Eckhardt in 1872, imagines Lee, who served as president of Washington College in Lexington after the war, at his great lieutenant's graveside. Jackson's remains (aside from his left arm, which remains buried on the Lacy estate a few miles west of Chancellorsville) were later relocated a few yards away in what is now Stonewall Jackson Memorial Cemetery to where they now rest under the monument on the right. (Library of Congress/Shutterstock)*

following morning, it was taken to the Capitol, where an estimated 20,000 people made the trek to pay their respects to the fallen warrior. Few were immune to the sense of shock that swept over the Confederacy during those days. "You must forgive me," President Jefferson Davis was forced to remark to a friend at one point, "I am still staggering from a dreadful blow. I cannot think."

After a private memorial service on the May 13 at the Virginia governor's mansion, Jackson began his final journey back to Lexington. Traveling by train to Gordonsville, and from there on to Lynchburg, the casket then traveled by water the rest of the way to Lexington. All along the route, residents came out by the thousands to pay their respects. At Lexington, the superintendent of VMI, Col. Francis Smith, greeted the boat when it arrived on May 14 and arranged with Anna for a funeral service the following day. The entire corps of cadets was on hand to escort Jackson's casket back to VMI, where it would rest in one of his old classrooms.

On May 15, the funeral service was held in the town's Presbyterian Church, with an estimated 4,000 people in attendance. Finally, at around noon, the service ended. With a seemingly endless line of cadets, veterans, and local dignitaries serving as escort, the body of Thomas J. Jackson traveled to the cemetery where it was finally laid to rest.

AFTERWORD

Stonewall Jackson was gone, but the Civil War would last two more terrible, bloody years. During that time, Confederate fortunes experienced a steady decline, until final defeat came with the surrender of Lee's army in April 1865 and the rest of the Confederate armed forces shortly thereafter. In light of the fact that the history of the war east of the Appalachians prior to May 1863 was one in which Confederate arms were successful more often than not, while the converse is true of the war after that point, it is not surprising that Jackson's death is widely seen as a major turning point in the war, the point when fortune turned decisively against the South in its bid for independence. Thus, the question of how history would have been different had Jackson and his talents been available to Lee at the great battle the Army of Northern Virginia fought less than two months after Jackson's death at Gettysburg, or at any number of future battlefields, has naturally prompted considerable discussion and debate. How would the course and outcome of the campaigns and battles that were fought at Gettysburg, Bristoe Station, the Wilderness, or Cold Harbor—not to mention the war as a whole—have been different had Lee and his army had the benefit of Jackson's leadership? Would still having Jackson been enough to enable the South to achieve its independence?

There is, of course, no truly satisfactory answer to these questions. The course and outcome of all military operations are the product of innumerable contingencies in which the ability or lack thereof of a particular commander is but one of many factors on which the course and outcome of events hinge. While undoubtedly a general of considerable ability, Jackson recognized that the question of victory or defeat at such places as Manassas, Kernstown, Harpers Ferry, and Fredericksburg was determined by innumerable factors over which he had little direct control. Indeed, a recognition of the degree to which the course of events was beyond any one individual's control undoubtedly did much to fuel the zeal with which Jackson sought and hoped for divine assistance to his efforts.

Still, there is no doubt that Jackson's death was a terrible blow to the Confederate cause in Virginia. His leadership during the first two years of the war had been critical to the Confederacy's ability to win victories on such battlefields as Manassas, Harpers Ferry, and Fredericksburg. Defeats at any one of these battles would have had devastating consequences for the cause of Confederate independence and undoubtedly would have accelerated the arrival of Union victory. Above all, though, it was the great campaign in the Shenandoah Valley in the spring of 1862 where Jackson's greatness as a general and importance to the Confederacy were most evident. In addition to offering a superb demonstration of generalship that has few equals in American military history, the boldness and brilliance of Jackson's operations in the Shenandoah Valley in the spring of 1862 led Federal authorities to commit major blunders that compromised the great campaign against Richmond on which whatever hopes of quickly bringing the war in Virginia to a triumphant end for Union arms rested.

To be sure, Jackson made his fair share of mistakes as a general. In the Romney Campaign the very qualities that made him successful elsewhere—his powerful will and belief in the virtue of always aggressively conducting operations—led him to push beyond the point where anything could be accomplished that would compensate for the toll winter campaigning took on his command. At Kernstown, those same qualities led him into a near disaster, although this was spectacularly

redeemed by the larger-than-life impression his actions made on authorities in Washington. His poor performances during the Seven Days
Battles, while an understandable product of fatigue, likewise had significant consequences for Confederate arms in that they killed whatever slim hopes Lee's army had to achieve a complete victory outside
Richmond in the summer of 1862. Nonetheless, on the whole there is
no question that Jackson's positive contributions to the Confederate
war effort far, far outweighed these black marks on an otherwise stellar
military record.

In fact, the failure of the Confederate bid for independence was the
product of both defeat on the battlefield and larger economic, social,
and political forces. While these were in many ways intertwined, and
Jackson's great ability as a field commander could and did have profound effects on the battlefields of the Eastern Theater and the deci-
sions of strategists in Washington and Richmond, the larger forces at
work were largely beyond his control. There is little doubt, though, that
Jackson's presence would have made the military history of the last two
years of the war even more interesting than they were and provided
plenty more grist for the mill of history.

FURTHER READING

As with all major Civil War military leaders, the literature on Jackson is extensive, with multiple studies of his life and campaigns available for those interested in studying those subjects in greater depth. By far the best biography of Jackson is James I. Robertson Jr.'s massive and magnificent *Stonewall Jackson: The Man, the Soldier, the Legend* (1997). Robertson's work is one of the truly outstanding works of Civil War biography and one for which there are simply not enough superlatives to do it justice. For those daunted by its mass, there are a number of other very good shorter, but still quite substantial, biographies. Prior to the appearance of Robertson's work, the best study of Jackson's life was *Mighty Stonewall* (1957) by Frank E. Vandiver, one of the 20th century's great American military historians. Other notable biographical treatments include Byron Farwell, *Stonewall: A Biography of General Thomas J. Jackson* (1993), G.F.R. Henderson, *Stonewall Jackson and the Civil War* (2 vols., 1899), and staff officer Robert L. Dabney's *Life and Campaigns of Lieut.-Gen. Thomas J. Jackson* (1866). Excellent sources for primary source material from Jackson's life and military career include Mary Anna Jackson's *Life and Letters of General Thomas J. Jackson* (1891), and U.S. War Department, *The War of the Rebellion: A*

Compilation of the Official Records of the Union and Confederate Armies (70 vols. in 128 parts; 1880–1901).

Excellent, more recent works have been produced on many of the officers with whom Jackson served. The most notable study of Robert E. Lee's life and military career remains Douglas Southall Freeman's *R. E. Lee: A Biography* (4 vols., 1934–35). Excellent, but more recent, works on Lee include Emory M. Thomas, *Robert E. Lee: A Biography* (1995), Gary W. Gallagher, ed., *Lee the Soldier* (1995), Elizabeth Brown Pryor, *Reading the Man: A Portrait of Robert E. Lee through His Private Letters* (2007), and Brian Holden Reid, *Robert E. Lee: Icon for a Nation* (2007). Freeman's *Lee's Lieutenants: A Study in Command* (3 vols., 1942–44) is a landmark study of the men who served the Confederate cause in Virginia.

The officers Jackson served under at First Manassas are the subject of Craig L. Symonds, *Joseph E. Johnston: A Civil War Biography* (1994) and T. Harry Williams, *P.G.T. Beauregard: Napoleon in Gray* (1955). The man who was perhaps Jackson's best subordinate officer is the subject of a fittingly outstanding biography: Donald C. Pfanz's *Richard S. Ewell: A Soldier's Life* (1998). Other excellent studies of men who served with and under Jackson are James I. Robertson Jr., *General A. P. Hill: The Story of a Confederate Warrior* (1987); Hal Bridges, *Lee's Maverick General: Daniel Harvey Hill* (1961); Jeffry D. Wert, *General James Longstreet, the Confederacy's Most Controversial Commander: A Biography* (1993); Thomas M. Settles, *John Bankhead Magruder: A Military Reappraisal* (2009); T. Michael Parrish, *Richard Taylor: Soldier Prince of Dixie* (1992); Jeffry D. Wert, *Cavalryman of the Lost Cause: A Biography of J.E.B. Stuart* (2009); and Paul Christopher Anderson, *Blood Image: Turner Ashby in the Civil War and the Southern Mind* (2003). The history of the unit that won fame with Jackson and served as the backbone of his various commands is effectively chronicled in James I. Robertson Jr., *The Stonewall Brigade* (1963).

All of the major military operations Jackson participated in have been the subject of focused studies. Understandably overshadowed by the Civil War, the Mexican-American War has nonetheless been the subject of a number of fine works. Very good overall surveys are provided in K. Jack Bauer, *The Mexican War, 1846–48* (1974), and John S. D. Eisenhower, *So Far from God: The U.S. War with Mexico*

1846–1848 (1989). Timothy D. Johnson provides a fine account of the campaign that captured Mexico City in *A Gallant Little Army: The Mexico City Campaign* (2007).

The best military history of the Civil War remains Herman Hattaway and Archer Jones, *How the North Won: A Military History of the Civil War* (1983), while Confederate strategy during the first year and a half of the war is magnificently and efficiently examined in Joseph L. Harsh, *Confederate Tide Rising: Robert E. Lee and the Making of Southern Strategy, 1861–1862* (1998).

The outstanding study of the Battle of First Manassas (or Bull Run) is John Hennessy, *The First Battle of Manassas: An End to Innocence, July 18–21, 1861* (1989), while the story of the campaign as a whole is effectively told in William C. Davis, *Battle at Bull Run: A History of the First Major Campaign of the Civil War* (1977), Ethan S. Rafuse, *A Single Grand Victory: The First Campaign and Battle of Manassas* (2002), David Detzer, *Donnybrook: The Battle of Bull Run, 1861* (2004), and Bradley M. Gottfried, *The Maps of First Bull Run: An Atlas of the First Bull Run (Manassas) Campaign, including the Battle of Ball's Bluff, June–October 1861* (2009).

The Romney Campaign is the focus of Thomas M. Rankin, *Stonewall Jackson's Romney Campaign: January 1–February 20, 1862* (1994). It is also addressed in two outstanding studies of the 1862 Shenandoah Valley Campaign: Robert G. Tanner, *Stonewall in the Valley: Thomas J. "Stonewall" Jackson's Shenandoah Valley Campaign, Spring 1862* (1976), and Peter Cozzens, *Shenandoah 1862: Stonewall Jackson's Valley Campaign* (2008). Excellent essays on the campaign can be found in Gary W. Gallagher, ed., *The Shenandoah Valley Campaign of 1862* (2003), while treatments of particular engagements are provided in two first-rate studies by Gary Ecelbarger: *"We Are In for It!": The First Battle of Kernstown, March 23, 1862* (1997), and *Three Days in the Shenandoah: Stonewall Jackson at Front Royal and Winchester* (2008), as well as Richard L. Armstrong, *Battle of McDowell* (1991), and Robert K. Krick, *Conquering the Valley: Stonewall Jackson at Port Republic* (1996).

The best study of the Peninsula Campaign and Seven Days Battles as a whole is Stephen W. Sears, *To the Gates of Richmond: The Peninsula Campaign* (1992), while very good essays on aspects of these operations are provided in William J. Miller, ed., *The Peninsula Campaign of 1862* (3 vols., 1995–97), and Gary W. Gallagher, ed., *The Richmond Campaign of 1862* (2000). Brian K. Burton's *Extraordinary Circumstances: The Seven Days Battles* (2001) is an outstanding focused study of the battles in front of Richmond. Those who wish to visit the sites where the course and outcome of the Peninsula Campaign were shaped, a task that is essential to any effort to fully understand any military operation, will find Burton's *The Peninsula and Seven Days: A Battlefield Guide* (2007) invaluable.

The operations in central and northern Virginia in August 1862 that transferred the war from the gates of Richmond to the outskirts of Washington are best chronicled in John J. Hennessy, *Return to Bull Run: The Campaign and Battle of Second Manassas* (1993), a magnificently executed work whose quality has rarely been matched by any other Civil War campaign study. The hard-fought engagement at Cedar Mountain that preceded the Second Manassas Campaign is authoritatively recounted in Robert K. Krick, *Stonewall Jackson at Cedar Mountain* (1990), while the fight at Ox Hill (Chantilly) is examined in David A. Welker, *Tempest at Ox Hill: The Battle of Chantilly* (2002). Second Manassas and the subsequent Maryland Campaign are studied together in Benjamin F. Cooling, *Counter-Thrust: From the Peninsula to the Antietam* (2007).

Although its focus is on the Confederate side, the outstanding study of the Maryland Campaign is Joseph L. Harsh, *Taken at the Flood: Robert E. Lee and Confederate Strategy in the Maryland Campaign of 1862* (1999). Readers will also find value in Stephen W. Sears, *Landscape Turned Red: The Battle of Antietam* (1983), and two collections of essays edited by Gary W. Gallagher: *Antietam: Essays on the 1862 Maryland Campaign* (1989), and *The Antietam Campaign* (1999). Ethan S. Rafuse, *Antietam, South Mountain, and Harpers Ferry: A Battlefield Guide* (2008), will be useful to those who wish to visit the Maryland Campaign battlefields.

George C. Rable offers an outstanding study of the Fredericksburg Campaign in all of its aspects in *Fredericksburg! Fredericksburg!* (2002). Rable's work is superbly complemented by Francis Augustin O' Reilly's stellar, but more militarily focused *The Fredericksburg Campaign: Winter War on the Rappahannock* (2003). Fredericksburg is studied together with Chancellorsville in Daniel E. Sutherland's excellent

Fredericksburg and Chancellorsville: The Dare Mark Campaign (1998), while Stephen W. Sears offers an exceptionally effective study of Jackson's last battle in *Chancellorsville* (1996). Gary W. Gallagher has edited excellent collections of essays on both battles: *The Fredericksburg Campaign: Decision on the Rappahannock* (1995), and *Chancellorsville: The Battle and Its Aftermath* (1996).

Other works that cannot be classified as biographies or campaign studies, but nonetheless offer interesting perspectives and insights on Jackson's life and career include Charles Royster, *The Destructive War: William Tecumseh Sherman, Stonewall Jackson, and the Americans* (1991), and John C. Waugh, *The Class of 1846: From West Point to Appomattox: Stonewall Jackson, George McClellan, and Their Brothers* (1994). Readers will also find consistently intriguing and provocative takes on Jackson and related topics in Confederate military history in the essays contained in Robert K. Krick, *The Smoothbore Volley that Doomed the Confederacy: The Death of Stonewall Jackson and Other Chapters on the Army of Northern Virginia* (2002), and A. Wilson Greene, *Whatever You Resolve to Be: Essays on Stonewall Jackson* (2005).

INDEX

About the Author

ETHAN S. RAFUSE is professor of military history at the U.S. Army Command and General Staff College at Fort Leavenworth, Kansas. He is the author of several books, including *A Single Grand Victory: The First Campaign and Battle of Manassas*, *McClellan's War: The Failure of Moderation in the Struggle for the Union*, and *Robert E. Lee and the Fall of the Confederacy, 1863–1865*.